The World's Greatest Collection of

Heavenly Humor

Compiled by
BOB PHILLIPS

HARVEST HOUSE PUBLISHERS
Eugene, Oregon 97402

**THE WORLD'S GREATEST COLLECTION
OF HEAVENLY HUMOR**

Copyright © 1982 Harvest House Publishers
Eugene. Oregon 97402
Library of Congress Number: 81-82676
ISBN 0-89081-297-7

Printed in the United States of America

ACCUSATION

A member of the church came to the pastor and said: "Pastor, my six brethren are all asleep, and I alone have remained awake to worship God."

The pastor replied, "You would be better off asleep if your worship of God consists of accusations against your brethren."

ACTIVE

Visitor: Pastor, how many of your members are active?

Pastor: They all are! Some are active for the Lord and the rest are active for the devil!

ADAM

The only things Adam would recognize if he came back to earth are the jokes.

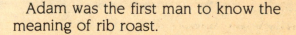

Adam was the first man to know the meaning of rib roast.

Adam was rejected for Eden the apple.

What a good thing Adam had. When he said something he knew nobody had said it before.

Adam may have had his troubles, but at least he didn't have to listen to Eve talking about the man she could have married.

The first Adam-splitting gave us Eve, a force which ingenious men in all ages have never gotten under control.

Eve was nigh Adam; Adam was naive.

Eve: Adam, do you love me?
Adam: Who else?

Conversation between Adam and Eve must have been difficult at times because they had nobody to talk about.

———■———

Eve was the first person who ate herself out of house and home.

———■———

Adam and Eve were the first book-keepers; they invented the loose-leaf system.

———■———

Adam and Eve lived thousands of years B.C.—before clothing.

———■———

Adam and Eve in the Garden of Eden couldn't complain how much better things were in the good old days.

———■———

Even Adam and Eve had their problems. One day Adam got angry. "You've done it again, Eve," said Adam, "You put my shirt in the salad again."

And here are Adam and Eve living together in Paradise. You can tell it's Paradise. Not once does Eve ask Adam to take out the garbage.

━■━

You remember Eve, the first woman who ever said: "I haven't got a thing to wear" and meant it!

━■━

Whatever other problems poor Adam may have faced, he at least never had to listen to Eve complain about other women having finer clothes than she.

━■━

When Eve tried to get out of the Garden without him, Adam called up to the Commanding Officer, "Eve is absent without leaf!"

━■━

Weary salesclerk: "Did you ever wonder how many fig leaves Eve tried on before she said, 'I'll take this one'?"

This country doesn't need a third party; it was a third party that spoiled things in the Garden of Eden.

———

The Bible begins with a man and a woman in a garden and it ends with the Revelation.

———

Question: At what season did Eve eat the fruit?
Answer: Early in the fall.

———

Question: What nationality were Adam and Eve?
Answer: Soviet citizens, of course . . . nothing to wear, only an apple to eat but living in Paradise.

———

Question: What was Eve's telephone number in the Garden of Eden?
Answer: I think it was Adam-812.

Question: How were Adam and Eve prevented from gambling?

Answer: Their paradise (pair-o-dice) was taken away from them.

Question: What is that which Adam never saw or possessed, yet left two for each of his children?

Answer: Parents.

Question: What is the first theatrical event the Bible mentions?

Answer: Eve's appearance for Adam's benefit.

Question: Who was the fastest runner in the world?

Answer: Adam, because he was first in the human race.

Question: What did Adam and Eve do when they were expelled from Eden?

Answer: They raised Cain.

Question: At what time of day was Adam born?

Answer: A little before Eve.

—■—

Question: Why had Eve no fear of the measles?

Answer: Because she'd Adam.

—■—

Question: Why was Adam's first day the longest?

Answer: Because it had no Eve.

—■—

Question: Who introduced the first walking stick?

Answer: Eve—when she presented Adam a little Cain.

—■—

Question: Who was created first, Adam or Eve?

Answer: Eve. She was the first maid.

When God performed the first marriage in the garden of Eden, it was between Adam and Eve not Adam and Steve.

—■—

The little rich girl came back from her first trip to Sunday school and told her mother, ''Oh, Mummy! They read us the nicest story! All about a Mr. Adam and a Miss Eve and what a nice time they were having under an apple tree until a servant came along and disturbed them.''

—■—

Sam: My daddy has a sword of Washington and a hat of Lincoln.
Bill: My father has an Adam's apple.

—■—

Sunday school Teacher: Class, what do you know about Adam's wife, Eve?
Student: They name Christmas Eve after her.

A Sunday school teacher asked Little Willie who the first man in the Bible was.

"Hoss," said Willie.

"Wrong," said the teacher. "It was Adam."

"Ah, shucks!" Willie replied. "I knew it was one of those Cartwrights."

———◼———

A Sunday school teacher asked her class to draw a picture illustrating a Bible story. One paper handed in contained a picture of a big car. An old man, with long whiskers flying in the breeze, was driving. A man and a woman were seated in the back of the car. Puzzled, the teacher asked little Johnny to explain his drawing. "Why, that is God. He is driving Adam and Eve out of the Garden of Eden."

———◼———

The little girl reported at home what she had learned at Sunday school concerning the creation of Adam and Eve: "The teacher told us how God made the first man and the first woman. He made the man first. But the man was very lonely with nobody to talk to him. So God put the man to sleep. And while the man was asleep, God took out his brains and made a woman of them."

Surgeon: I think the medical profession is the first profession mentioned in the Bible. God made Eve by carving a rib out of Adam.

Engineer: No, engineering was first. Just think of the engineering job it was to create things out of chaos.

Politician: That's nothing . . . Who do you think created chaos?

—■—

Sunday school teacher: Can anyone tell me the story of Adam and Eve?

Little girl: First God created Adam. Then He looked at him and said, "I think I could do better if I tried again." So He created Eve.

—■—

After hearing the story about how God took the rib out of Adam's side, a little boy who had been running and had gotten a sideache replied to his mother: "I think I'm going to have a wife."

—■—

AIR-CONDITIONED

"Our church should be air-conditioned," snapped Mrs. Smith. "It is unhealthy for people to sleep in a stuffy room."

AGNOSTIC

Agnostic is Latin for ignoramus.

———■———

Agnostic . . . A learned man who doesn't pretend to know what ignorant men are sure of.

———■———

Agnostic . . . That's what you beat an agno with.

———■———

Agnostic . . . A person who says that he knows nothing about God and, when you agree with him, he becomes angry.

———■———

Agnostic: If those Christians would stop building such large and fancy buildings and give the money to the poor it would be more to their credit.
Christian: I've heart that remark before.
Agnostic: Indeed! And by whom, may I ask?
Christian: Judas Iscariot.

AMEN

Mack: Why do you say "amen" in a church instead of "awomen"?

Jack: Because you sing hymns, not hers.

■

We've been letting our six-year-old go to sleep listening to the radio, and I'm beginning to wonder if it's a good idea. Last night he said his prayers and wound up with: "And God bless Mommy and Daddy and Sister. Amen—and FM!"

■

The sermon went on and on and on in the heat of the church. At last the minister paused and asked, "What more, my friends, can I say?"

In the back of the church a voice offered earnestly: "Amen!"

■

The new Army recruit was given guard duty at 2 a.m. He did his best for awhile but about 4 a.m. he went to sleep. He awakened to find the officer of the day standing before him.

Remembering the heavy penalty for being asleep on guard duty, this smart young man kept his head bowed for another moment, then looked upward and reverently said, "A-a-a-men!"

AMUSEMENT

Henry Ward Beecher asked Park Benjamin, the poet and humorist, why he never came to hear him preach. Benjamin replied, "Why, Beecher, the fact is I have conscientious scruples against going to places of amusement on Sunday."

ANGELS

God made man a little lower than the angels, and he has been getting a little lower ever since.

—Will Rogers

A woman who is always up in the air and harping on something is not necessarily an angel.

A conscientious minister decided to get acquainted with a new family in his congregation and called on them one spring evening. After his knock on the door, a lilting voice from within called out, "Is that you, Angel?" "No," replied the minister, "but I'm from the same department."

A girl whose father was a photographer was out fishing with her parents one afternoon when a sudden storm came up and there was a brilliant flash. "Look," she said. "The angels are taking pictures of us!"

APOCRYPHAL

Hippety-hop to the corner shop for apocryphal of candy.

APPROPRIATE

It was a formal banquet. The minister had just finished saying grace when a waiter spilled a bowl of steaming soup into his lap. The clergyman silently sizzled, then said in anguished tones: "Will some layman please make some appropriate remarks?"

ARK

Ark: injunction to listen, as in "Ark, I think it's raining!"

ART

"It's no use. Art doesn't listen to me," said a little boy who was praying for a bike. "Art who?" asked the boy's mother. "Art in heaven," came the reply.

ARMAGEDDON

Ad in newspaper:
Armageddon—The Earth's Last War—
 How and Where It Will Be Fought
  At the First Baptist Church

As St. John said after his dream, "Armageddon out of here!"

In biblical days it was considered a miracle for an ass to speak; now it would be a miracle if one kept quiet.

ATHEIST

An atheist is one who hopes the Lord will do nothing to disturb his disbelief.
                    —Franklin P. Jones

An atheist is one point beyond the devil.

—◼—

The chief fault with atheism is that it has no future.

—◼—

An atheist is a man who has no invisible means of support.

—◼—

Atheism—The three great apostles of practical atheism that make converts without persecuting, and retain them without preaching, are health, wealth, and power.

—Colton

—◼—

To be an atheist requires an infinitely greater measure of faith than to receive all the great truths which atheism would deny.

—Joseph Addison

—◼—

No atheist can injure the Bible's influence so thoroughly as a Christian who disregards it in his daily life.

You can always tell an atheist during the Crusades. They were the ones who wanted to negotiate.

—■—

How to wipe out an atheist: Serve him a meal and then ask him if he believes there is a cook.

—■—

Did you hear about the son of the atheists who asked his parents: "Do you think God knows we don't believe in him?"

—■—

Overheard: "I'm an atheist, thank God."

—■—

Atheists are really on the spot: They have to sing "Hmmmmmm bless America."

—■—

An atheist is a disbeliever who prefers to raise his children in a Christian community.

Sign on the tomb of an atheist:
HERE LIES AN ATHEIST ALL DRESSED UP
AND NO PLACE TO GO.

━■━

They have all sorts of new services today. Now they've got a dial-a-prayer service for atheists. You call a number and
nobody answers.

━■━

Pity the poor atheist who feels grateful
but has no one to thank.

━■━

The atheist cannot find God for the same
reason that a thief cannot find a
policeman.

━■━

I once wanted to become an atheist but I
gave up the idea. They have no holidays.

━■━

All atheists pray at times when they can
find no other way out of their troubles.

Atheism is rather in the life than in the heart of man.

—Francis Bacon

Atheism is the death of hope, the suicide of the soul.

Nobody talks so constantly about God as those who insist that there is no God.

Some are atheists only in fair weather.

I feel sorry for an atheist who needs help How do you pray to Charles Darwin?

An atheist is a man who looks through a telescope and tries to explain all that he can't see.

An atheist was teasing Bill about his religious beliefs. "Come on now, Bill," he said, "Do you really believe that when you die you'll go up to heaven and fly around with wings? I understand it's not warm up there like where I'm going when I die. How in the world are you going to get your coat on over those wings?"

Bill replied, "The same way you are going to get your trousers over your tail!"

Three atheists were trying to bother a young Baptist minister.

"I think I will move to Nevada," said the first atheist. "Only twenty-five percent of the people are Baptists."

"No, I think I would rather live in Colorado," said the second man; "Only ten percent of the people are Baptists."

"Better yet," said the third atheist, "is New Mexico . . . only five percent there are Baptists."

"I think the best place for you all is Hades," said the minister. "There are no Baptists there!"

Atheist: Do you honestly believe that Jonah spent three days and nights in the belly of a whale?

Preacher: I don't know, sir, but when I get to heaven I'll ask him.

Atheist: But suppose he isn't in heaven?

Preacher: Then you ask him!

ATTENDANCE

"Does your husband attend church regularly?"

"Oh, yes. He hasn't missed an Easter Sunday since we were married."

AWAKE

Many churches are now serving coffee after the sermon. Presumably this is to get the people thoroughly awake before they drive home.

BABEL

The Tower of Babel was a din of iniquity.

BABY

Billy watched his new baby sister in the crib as she screamed and kicked. He finally asked, "Where did she come from?"

"Heaven," was the reply. "No wonder they let her go," Billy responded

BALAAM

"I am thankful that the Lord has opened my mouth to preach without any larning," said an illiterate preacher.

"A similar event took place in Balaam's time," replied a gentleman present.

BAPTISM

I don't mind going to a church service in a drive-in theater. But when they hold the baptisms in a car wash, that's going too far!

BAPTIST

Q. When you have fifty people all of different opinions, what do you have?

A. A Baptist church.

"You're a minister, huh?"

"Yes, I am."

"What church?"

"Baptist."

"Oh, you're the narrow-minded bunch that believes only their group is going to make it to heaven."

"I'm even more narrow-minded than that. I don't think all of our group is going to make it!"

—◼—

"Some people say the Baptist denomination started with John the Baptist, but it was much earlier than that," said a great Baptist leader as he spoke to a large gathering of Baptist ministers. "In fact, it started way over in the Old Testament. In the 13th chapter of Genesis, it says Lot said to Abraham, 'You go your way and I'll go mine.' That's when the Baptists began."

—◼—

"Baptist fellowship is heavenly."

"Yeah, heaven is the only place it will work."

A Baptist deacon had advertised a cow for sale.

"How much are you asking for it?" inquired a prospective purchaser.

"A hundred and fifty dollars," said the advertiser.

"And how much milk does she give?"

"Four gallons a day," he replied.

"But how do I know that she will actually give that amount?" asked the purchaser.

"Oh, you can trust me," reassured the advertiser. "I'm a Baptist deacon."

"I'll buy it," replied the other. "I'll take the cow home and bring you back the money later. You can trust me, I'm a Presbyterian elder."

When the deacon arrived home he asked his wife, "What is a Presbyterian elder?"

"Oh," she explained, "a Presbyterian elder is about the same as a Baptist deacon."

"Oh, dear," groaned the deacon, "I have just lost my cow!"

A Presbyterian minister was about to baptize a baby. Turning to the father, he inquired, "His name, please?"

"William Patrick Arthur Timothy John MacArthur."

The minister turned to his assistant and said, "A little more water, please."

Several churches in the South decided to hold union services. The leader was a Baptist and proud of his denomination.

"How many Baptists are here?" he asked on the first night of the revival.

All except one little lady raised their hands.

"Lady, what are you?" asked the leader.

"I'm a Methodist," meekly replied the lady.

"Why are you a Methodist?" queried the leader.

"Well," replied the little old lady, "my grandparents were Methodists, my mother was a Methodist, and my late husband was a Methodist.'

"Well," retorted the leader, "just supposing all your relatives had been morons, what would that have made you?"

"Oh, I see. A Baptist, I suppose," the lady replied meekly.

Two Chinamen were heard discussing the denominational difference between the Baptists, Methodists and English Friends. One of them said to the other:

"They say these denominations have different beliefs. Just what is the difference between them?"

"Oh," said the other, "not much! Big washee, little washee, and no washee, that is all."

A Methodist and Baptist were arguing the virtues of their baptisms. The Methodist said, "All right, if I take a man and lead him in the water to his ankles, is he baptized?"

"No."

" 'Til just the top of his head is showing above the water, is he baptized?"

"No," said the Baptist.

"All right, then," asserted the Methodist. "That's where we baptize them."

BASEBALL

Baseball is talked about a great deal in the Bible: In the big inning, Eve stole first—Adam stole second—Gideon rattled the pitchers—Goliath was put out by David—and the Prodigal Son made a home run.

———◼———

BEGORRA

Begorra . . . This word, says The Oxford Dictionary, is an Irish corruption. That probably explains why there is a Dublin bar for homosexuals called Sodom and Begorra.

———◼———

BELIEF

A preacher once asked an actor why he had such large audiences and he, the preacher, had only a small audience at church.

"I act as if I believe in what I say," said the actor, "while you preach as if you did not believe what you preached."

———◼———

Philosopher Bertrand Russell, asked if he was willing to die for his beliefs, replied: "Of course not. After all, I may be wrong."

One person with a belief is equal to a force of ninety-nine who have only interests.

Strong beliefs win strong men, and then make them stronger.

BELIEVE

Joe: Say, what do you believe about God?

Moe: I believe what my church believes.

Joe: What does your church believe?

Moe: My church believes what I believe.

Joe: What do you and your church believe?

Moe: We both believe the same thing.

BETTER WORK

The kid said, "Dad, did God make you?"

"Yes."

"Did he make me?"

"Yes."

"Doing better work lately, eh?"

BIBLE

The family Bible can be passed down from generation to generation because it gets so little wear.

∎

The Scriptures teach us the best way of living, the noblest way of suffering, and the most comfortable way of dying.

—Flavel

∎

Most people are bothered by those passages of Scripture they do not understand, but the passages that bother me are those I do understand.

—Mark Twain

∎

The man who samples the Word of God occasionally never acquires much of a taste for it.

The Bible is a window in this prison-world, through which we may look into eternity.

—Timothy Dwight

Nobody ever outgrows Scripture; the book widens and deepens with our years.

—Spurgeon

It is an awful responsibility to own a Bible.

Be careful how you live; you may be the only Bible some person ever reads.

Men do not usually reject the Bible because it contradicts itself, but because it contradicts them.

Dust on your Bible is not evidence that it is a dry book.

———■———

A Bible stored in the mind is worth a dozen stored in the bottom of one's trunk.

———■———

One of the best evidences of the inspiration and infallibility of the Bible is that it has survived the fanaticism of its friends.

———■———

If all the neglected Bibles in this country were dusted off at the same time, we would suffer the worst dust storm we have experienced in many years.

———■———

The reason people are down on the Bible is that they're not up on the Bible.
                              —William Ward Ayer

Sin will keep you from this Book. This Book will keep you from sin.

—Dwight L. Moody

Johnny: Mother's Bible must be more interesting than yours.

Father: Why do you say that?

Johnny: She reads it more than you read yours.

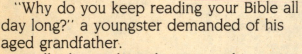

"Why do you keep reading your Bible all day long?" a youngster demanded of his aged grandfather.

"Well," he explained, "you might say I was cramming for my final examinations."

BIGOTS

There are two kinds of people in your church: Those who agree with you and the bigots.

BINGO

I've always been fascinated by churches that run bingo games. It's like, out front they ought to have a sign: COME LET US PREY.

—■—

BLINDNESS

During church services an attractive young widow leaned too far over the balcony and fell, but her dress caught on a chandelier and held her suspended in mid-air. The minister, of course, immediately noticed the woman's predicament and called out to his congregation: "The first person who looks up there is in danger of being punished with blindness."

One old fellow in the congregation whispered to the man next to him, "I think I'll risk one eye.'

—■—

BELLY BUTTON

Bill: How do babies get their belly buttons?

Suzzie: Well, when God finishes making little babies, He lines them all up in a row. Then he walks along in front of them, pokes each one in the tummy with His finger, and says, "You're done . . . you're done . . . and you're done."

BOOKIE

Pastor: How do you like your job as church librarian?

Librarian: It is all right as long as people call me a librarian and not a bookie.

BORED

After a long, dry sermon, the minister announced that he wished to meet with the church board following the close of the service. The first man to arrive was a stranger. "You misunderstood my announcement. This is a meeting of the board," said the minister.

"I know," said the man, "but if there is anyone here more bored than I am, I'd like to meet him."

BOWLING

Did you hear the one about the ministers who formed a bowling team? Called themselves the Holy Rollers.

BRIDEGROOM

The bridegroom, who was in a horribly nervous condition, appealed to the clergyman in a loud whisper, at the close of the ceremony:

"Is it kisstomary to cuss the bride?"

The clergyman replied:

"Not yet, but soon."

BUDDHIST

A Buddhist nudist is one who practices yoga bare.

BUILDING FUND

I'm always suspicious of any church that tells you the end is near—and then asks you to sign a three-year Building Fund pledge.

BURNT OFFERINGS

Teacher: In our lesson today we have talked about the burnt offerings offered in the Old Testament. Why don't we have burnt offerings today?

Student: On account of air pollution.

CAIN

Heckler: Who was Cain's wife?

Preacher: I respect any seeker of knowledge, but I want to warn you, young man, don't risk being lost to salvation by too much inquiring after other men's wives.

—■—

Fay: How long a period of time did Cain hate his brother?

Ray: As long as he was Abel.

—■—

CANNIBALS

A resourceful missionary fell into the hands of a band of cannibals. "Going to eat me, I take it," said the missionary. "You wouldn't like me." He took out his pocketknife, sliced a piece from the calf of his leg, and handed it to the chief. "Try it and see for yourself," he urged. The chief took one bite, grunted and spat.

The missionary remained on the island fifty years. He had a cork leg.

—■—

Then there's the missionary the cannibal couldn't boil. He was a friar.

Sunday School Teacher: What message should the missionaries teach the cannibals?

Student: To be vegetarians.

—◼—

CHRISTIAN

If Christians would really live according to the teachings of Christ, as found in the Bible, all of India would be Christian today.

—Mahatma Gandhi

—◼—

If a man cannot be a Christian in the place where he is, he cannot be a Christian anywhere.

—Henry Ward Beecher

—◼—

Nobody can teach you how to be a Christian—you learn it on the job.

—◼—

Christian names are everywhere; Christian men are very rare.

The pagans do not know God, and love only the earth. The Jews know the true God, and love only the earth. The Christians know the true God, and do not love the earth.

—Blaise Pascal

—■—

There is one single fact which we may oppose to all the wit and argument of infidelity, namely, that no man ever repented of being a Christian on his death bed.

—■—

A Christian is like ripening corn; the riper he grows the more lowly he bends his head.

—■—

A Christian must carry something heavier on his shoulders than chips.

—■—

Christian: one who believes that the New Testament is a divinely inspired book admirably suited to the spiritual needs of his neighbors.

Three Kinds of Christians:

1. Rowboat Christians . . . have to be pushed wherever they go.
2. Sailboat Christians . . . always go with the wind.
3. Steamboat Christians . . . make up their mind where they ought to go, and go there regardless of wind or weather.

CHRISTIANITY

Christianity is bread for daily use, not cake for special occasions.

———

Christianity has not been tried and found; it has been found difficult and not tried.

—Chesterton

———

The trouble with some of us is that we have been inoculated with small doses of Christianity which keep us from catching the real thing.

———

CHRISTMAS

Christmas began in the heart of God. It is complete only when it reaches the heart of man.

It is good to be children sometimes, and never better than at Christmas, when its mighty Founder was a child Himself.

—Dickens

I passed one of those lots that sells Christmas trees. You know the kind. They're dedicated to the proposition that only God can make a tree and only man can make a buck!

There seems to be some question as to whether more gifts are exchanged on Christmas or the day after.

"For Christmas," a woman remarked to her friend, "I was visited by a jolly, bearded fellow with a big bag over his shoulder. My son came home from college with his laundry."

There's nothing like the Christmas season to put a little bounce in your checks.

During a Christmas play: "Not a preacher was stirring, not even a mouse."

———■———

A little boy excited about his part in the Christmas play came home and said:
"I got a part in the Christmas play!"
"What part?" asked his mother.
"I'm one of the three wise guys!" was the reply.

———■———

CHURCH
"Why don't you come to my church this next Sunday?"
"Because I belong to another abomination."

———■———

Church . . . A place where you encounter nodding acquaintances.

———■———

An usher went up to a man with his hat on in church and asked him to remove it.
"Thank goodness," said the man, "I thought that would do it. I've attended this church for months, and you are the first person who has spoken to me."

"If absence makes the heart grow fonder," said a minister, "a lot of folks must love our church."

I don't want to say it was a cold church, but the ushers were using ice skates.

I spoke in one church that was so small that when I took a bow I hit my head on the back pew.

The chief trouble with the church is that you and I are in it.

Wife: Did you see that hat Mrs. Jones wore to church?
Husband: No!
Wife: Did you see the new dress Mrs. Smith had on?
Husband: No!
Wife: A lot of good it does you to go to church!

You can always tell a church that isn't doing well. The Cadillac they raffle off is used.

———■———

Church . . . An organization supported by the husbands of its members.

———■———

Some go to church to take a walk;
Some go there to laugh and talk;
Some go there to meet a friend;
Some go there their time to spend;
Some go there to meet a lover;
Some go there a fault to cover;
Some go there for speculation;
Some go there for observation;
Some go there to doze and nod;
The wise go there to worship.

CHURCH ATTENDERS

DICTIONARY OF CHURCH ATTENDERS:

PILLARS—Worship regularly, giving time and money.

LEANERS—Use the church for funerals, baptisms, and marriages.

SPECIALS—Help and give occasionally for something that appeals to them.

ANNUALS—Dress up for Easter and come for Christmas programs.

SPONGES—Take all blessing and benefits, even the sacraments, but never give out anything themselves.

SCRAPPERS—Take offense and criticize.

CHURCHGOER

Q: What do you call a non-churchgoer?
A: A Seventh-Day Absentist.

CHURCH MEMBERS

Some church members who say, "Our Father," on Sunday go around the rest of the week acting like orphans.

Every church has, in addition to the brakeman, a construction and wrecking crew. To which do you belong? One of them for sure.

—■—

Every church has three classes of members: The workers, the jerkers, and the shirkers.

—■—

There are four classes of church members: The tired, the retired, the tiresome and the tireless.

—■—

It seems that some church members have been starched and ironed, but too few have been washed.

—■—

First Pastor: I hear you had a revival.
Second Pastor: Yes, we did.
First Pastor: How many additions did you have?
Second Pastor: We didn't have any additions but we had some blessed subractions.

CHURCH SIGNS

Come in and let us prepare you for your finals.

Let us take you to our Leader.

No matter how much you nurse a grudge it won't get better.

Pray up in advance.

We specialize in faith lifting.

Ask about our pray-as-you-go plan.

Start living to beat hell.

This church is prayer-conditioned.

Come early . . . if you want a back seat.

———————

David and Bathsheba . . . you've seen the movie, now read the book.

———————

Merry Christmas to our Christian friends. Happy Hanukkah to our Jewish friends. To our atheist friends . . . good luck.

———————

If some people lived up to their ideals they would be stooping.

———————

Everything you always wanted to know about heaven and hell, but were afraid to ask.

———————

Remember, it is more blessed to give than to receive. Besides, you don't have to write thank-you notes.

CLEANLINESS

Cleanliness is next to godliness, but in childhood it's next to impossible.

—◼—

CLEOPATRA

Cleopatra was the queen of denial.

—◼—

CLERGYMAN

Clergyman . . . One who still preaches against modern dress even though there's not enough left to talk about.

—◼—

COLLECTION

A young clergyman, fresh out of the seminary, thought it would help him in his career if he first took a job as a policeman for several months. He passed the physical examination and then took the oral examination to ascertain his alertness of mind and his ability to act quickly and wisely in an emergency.

Among other questions he was asked, "What would you do to disperse a frenzied crowd?"

He thought a moment and then said, "I would take up a collection."

COMMITTEES

If you want to kill any idea in the world today, get a committee working on it.

Never fear that machines may get too powerful. When they do, we can organize them into committees.

A committee is a group that keeps minutes and loses hours.

—Milton Berle

To get something done a committee should consist of three men, two of whom are absent.

Committee is a noun of multitude: signifying many, but not signifying much.

A certain congregation was about to erect a new church edifice. The building committee, in consecutive meetings, passed the fellowship resolutions:

1. We shall build a new church.
2. The new building is to be located on the site of the old one.
3. The material in the old building is to be used in the new one.
4. We shall continue to use the old building until the new one is completed.

CONCLUSION

Second wind is what some preachers get when they say, "And now in conclusion."

CONFESSION

Confess your sins to the Lord, and you will be forgiven; confess them to men, and you will be laughed at.

—Josh Billings

CONFESSIONAL

Have you heard of the new drive-in confessional? It is called, "Toot and tell."

CONSENT

If thou wouldst conquer thy weakness, thou must never gratify it. No man is compelled to evil: his consent only makes it his. It is no sin to be tempted, but to be overcome.

—William Penn

CONSCIENCE

A good conscience is a continual Christmas.

—Benjamin Franklin

A guilty conscience is the mother of invention.

—Carolyn Wells

A guilty conscience is a hell on earth and points to one beyond.

All too often a clear conscience is merely the result of a bad memory.

———■———

CONTRADICT
People do not usually reject the Bible because it contradicts itself, but because it contradicts them.

———■———

CONVENTION
The road to hell is paved with good conventions.

———■———

COOKS
Heaven sends us good meat but the devil sends us cooks.

———■———

COUGHING
Preacher: A lot of people must be sick with colds. There was sure a great deal of coughing during my sermon this morning.
Deacon: Those were time signals.

CRITICIZE

When the family returned from Sunday morning service, father criticized the sermon, daughter thought the choir's singing was off-key, and mother found fault with the organist's playing. The subject had to be dropped when the small boy of the family said, "But it was a good show for a nickel, don't you think, Dad?"

―■―

DAVID

Q: Do you know how you can tell that David was older than Goliath?

A: Because David rocked Goliath to sleep!

―■―

DEACON

Pastor: Say, Deacon, a mule died out in front of the church.

Deacon: Well, it's the job of you ministers to look after the dead. Why tell me?

Pastor: You're right; it is my job. But we always notify the next of kin.

DEAD CAT

A young mother was trying to comfort her daughter when her pet kitten died, saying, "Remember, dear, Fluffy is up in heaven now with God."

"But, mommy," the girl sobbed. "What in the world would God want with a dead cat?"

DEAD IN CHRIST

One pastor said that his church people would be the first to go up in the rapture. He gave his reason: "The Bible says: 'The dead in Christ shall rise first.' "

DEFECTS

The defects of a preacher are soon spied.

—Luther

DEPRAVITY

Arriving home for the holidays from reform school, a teenage delinquent called out, "Look, Mom, no depravities!"

DEVIL

Where God builds a church the devil builds a chapel.

———■———

An old Puritan said, if you are a child of God and you marry a child of the devil, you will be sure to have trouble with your father-in-law.

———■———

The devil is never too busy to rock the cradle of a sleeping saint.

———■———

The devil's traps are never set in the middle of God's road.

———■———

The devil is an artist. He paints sin in very attractive colors.

———■———

Talk of the devil, and his horns appear, says the proverb.

—Samuel Taylor Coleridge

Johnny: There's really no devil.

Billy: I know what you mean. It's just like Santa Claus. It's your father.

A man was going to attend a Halloween party dressed in the costume of the devil. On his way it began to rain so he darted into a church where a revival meeting was in progress.

At the sight of his devil's costume, people began to scatter through the doors and windows.

One lady got her coat sleeve caught on the arm of one of the seats and as the man came closer, she pleaded, "Satan, I've been a member of this church for twenty years, but I've really been on your side all the time."

While a revival was being conducted by a muscular preacher, he was disturbed by two young men that scoffed at everything they saw or heard.

He paused and asked them why they attended the meeting.

"We came to see miracles performed," impudently replied one of them.

Leaving the pulpit and walking quietly down the aisle, the minister seized one after the other by the collar and, as they disappeared out of the door, remarked:

"We don't perform miracles here, but we do cast out devils."

—■—

DEVOTIONS

Wife: Shall I wake you up when you finish your devotions, dear?

—■—

DIED

Pastor: Isn't this a beautiful church? Here is a plaque for the men who died in the service.

Man: Which one? . . . Morning or evening?

—■—

DISCIPLINE

A young businessman returned home after a tough day at the office and found his two daughters, both of about kindergarten age, acting up pretty boisterously. He gave them a moderately severe scolding and sent them off to bed. The next morning he found a note stuck on his bedroom door: "Be good to your children and they will be good to you. God."

DIVORCE

America still has more marriages than divorces, proving that preachers can still outtalk lawyers.

DOCTRINE

Any doctrine that will not bear investigation is not a fit tenant for the mind of an honest man.

DONKEY

An evangelist was speaking in a meeting when a heckler shouted, "Listen to him! And his father used to drive a wagon led by a donkey."

"That's right," said the evangelist, "and today my father and the wagon are gone. But I see we still have the donkey with us."

DRINKING

Drinker: What pastoral advice have you for drivers who drink?

Preacher: Jug not lest ye be jugged.

DROWNING

A prominent preacher was approached after Sunday morning services by an elderly lady who said in a tone of appreciation, "Bishop, you'll never know what your service meant to me. It was just like water to a drowning man!"

DROUGHT

A visitor to a drought-stricken area was engaged in conversation at the local store about the "no-rain" situation.

"You think the drought is bad here," the merchant observed, "But down south o'here a ways, they haven't had any for so long that the Baptists are sprinkling, the Methodists are using a damp cloth, and the Presbyterians are issuing rain checks!"

DUST

On the way home from church a little boy asked his mother, "Is it true, Mommy, that we are made of dust?"

"Yes, darling."

"And do we go back to dust again when we die?"

"Yes, dear."

"Well, Mommy, when I said my prayers last night and looked under the bed, I found someone who is either coming or going."

DYING

Old Pete was very close to dying but made a miraculous recovery. In the hospital his pastor came to visit him and the conversation went like this:

"Tell me, Pete, when you were so near death's door, did you feel afraid to meet your Maker?"

"No, Pastor," said Pete. "It was the other man I was afraid of!"

ELISHA

The minister was addressing a Sunday school class. He had taken for his theme the familiar one of the children who mocked Elisha on his journey to Bethel—how the youngsters taunted the poor old prophet and how they were punished when two she-bears came out of the wild and ate forty-and-two of them.

"And now, children," said the pastor, wishing to discover whether his talk had produced any moral effect, "what does this story show?"

"Please, sir," came from a little girl well down in the front, "it shows how many children two she-bears can hold."

— ■ —

Mark Twain was fond of telling the story of a small boy's account of Elisha in his less ingratiating mood.

"There was a prophet named Elisha. One day he was going up a mountainside. Some boys threw stones at him. He said, 'If you keep on throwing stones at me I'll set the bears on you and they'll eat you up.' And they did, and he did, and the bears did."

— ■ —

ELOQUENCE

God gave eloquence to some, brains to others.

— ■ —

ENEMIES

The Bible tells us to love our neighbors and also to love our enemies, probably because they are generally the same people.

The little young lady of the house, by way of punishment for some minor misdemeanor, was compelled to eat her dinner alone at a little table in a corner of the dining room. The rest of the family paid no attention to her presence until they heard her audibly praying over her repast with the words, "I thank thee, Lord, for preparing a table before me in the presence of mine enemies."

EPISTLES

Sunday school teacher: What are Epistles?

Student: I guess they are the wives of the Apostles.

EUTYCHUS

Pastor: What do we learn from the story of Eutychus, the young man who, listening to the preaching of the Apostle Paul, fell asleep and, falling out of a window, was taken up dead?

Member: Ministers should learn not to preach too long sermons.

EVIL

The greatest penalty of evildoing is to grow into the likeness of bad men, and, growing like them, to fly from the conversation of the good, and be cut off from them, and cleave to and follow after the company of the bad.

—Plato

To plan evil is as wrong as doing it.

—Proverbs 24:8

Supervising evil does not make it good.

FAITH

Minister: When in doubt, faith it.

If it wasn't for faith, there would be no living in this world; we couldn't even eat hash with any safety.

—Josh Billings

FALSE TEETH

At a Sunday school picnic the minister, while walking across a small footbridge, was seized with a fit of sneezing. His false teeth flew from his mouth and landed in the clear water in the middle of the stream. Much worried and embarrassed, the minister was preparing to remove his shoes and wade in after them when a dear little gray-haired grandmother appeared on the scene, carrying a well-filled dinner basket. When she discovered the minister's plight, she reached in her basket, removed a crisp, brown chicken leg, tied a string to it and tossed it into the water near the dentures. Quickly the teeth clamped into the chicken leg and were hauled to safety.

—◼—

FAULTS

Every person should have a special cemetery lot in which to bury the faults of friends and loved ones.

—◼—

FEAR

Fear is the tax that conscience pays to guilt.

Fear the man who fears not God.

——◼——

FEE

God cures, but the doctor takes the fee.

——◼——

FISHING

Two men fishing on Sunday morning were feeling pretty guilty, especially since the fish didn't bite. One said to the other, "I guess I should have stayed home and gone to church."

To which the other angler replied lazily, "I couldn't have gone to church anyway . . . my wife's sick in bed."

——◼——

A village pastor, who had a weakness for trout, preached against fishing on Sunday. The next day one of his members presented him with a fine string of fish and said, hesitatingly, "I guess I ought to tell you, parson, that those trout were caught on Sunday." The minister gazed appreciatively at the speckled trout, and said piously, "The fish aren't to blame for that."

FLIRTING

The minister arose to address his congregation. "There is a certain man among us today who is flirting with another man's wife. Unless he puts five dollars in the collection box, his name will be read from the pulpit."

When the collection plate came in, there were nineteen five-dollar bills, and a two-dollar bill with this note attached: "Other three pay day."

FLOWERS

Q. What do they do with the church flowers after Sunday services?

A. They take them to the people who are sick after the sermons.

FLYING

Mother: You shouldn't be flying that model airplane in the back yard on Sunday.

Johnny: Oh, it is all right to fly this one. It isn't a pleasure plane. It's a missionary plane going to the jungle.

FOOL

Heckler: If I ever had a son who was a fool, I'd make a preacher out of him.

Preacher: How come your father didn't send you to seminary?

———■———

Reverend Henry Ward Beecher entered Plymouth Church one Sunday and found several letters awaiting him. He opened one and found it contained the single word, "Fool." Quietly and with becoming seriousness, he announced to the congregation that fact in these words:

"I have known many an instance of a man writing a letter and forgetting to sign his name, but this is the only instance I have ever known of a man signing his name and forgetting to write the letter."

———■———

FOOT IN MOUTH

A missionary was suddenly surrounded by hostile-looking tribesmen in a South American jungle. Noting their poised spears and poisoned arrows, he knew he had to think of something quickly.

At that moment a plane flew overhead. "See that bird up there," said the missionary. "That's my friend. If you hurt me that bird hurt you!"

The chief took one glance at the sky, then answered, "That's no bird. That's a Boeing 747!"

—■—

FORGIVENESS

It is easier for the generous to forgive, than for the offender to ask for forgiveness.

—■—

It is easier to forgive an enemy than a friend.

—■—

There is no revenge so complete as forgiveness.

—Josh Billings

—■—

Always forgive your enemies—nothing annoys them so much.

—Oscar Wilde

Forgiveness is the fragrance the violet sheds on the heel that has crushed it.
—Mark Twain

Forgiving the unrepentant is like drawing pictures on water.

Doing an injury puts you below your enemy; revenging one makes you but even with him; forgiving it sets you above him.

"I can forgive, but I cannot forget," is only another way of saying, "I will not forgive." Forgiveness ought to be like a cancelled note torn in two, and burned up, so that it never can be shown against one.
—Henry Ward Beecher

The weak can never forgive. Forgiveness is the attribute of the strong.
—Mahatma Gandhi

FREEDOM

Man is really free only in God, the source of his freedom.

To some people religious freedom means the choice of churches which they may stay away from.

Those who expect to reap the blessings of freedom must, like men, undergo the fatigues of supporting it.

FIRST ROW

In a church where everybody sat toward the rear, a stranger walked in and took a front seat. After the service, the minister greeted the stranger and asked why he sat up front.

"I'm a bus driver," he replied, "and I came to learn how you succeed in getting people to move to the back."

FUNERAL

The preacher of a small church in a remote section of the country once preached a funeral service of one of the local mountaineers and he explained the deceased's position in the community thusly:

"Now, he wasn't what you call a good man, because he never gave his heart to the Lord; but he was what you'd call a respected sinner."

—■—

A young minister, in the first days of his first parish, was obliged to call upon the widow of an eccentric man who had just died. Standing before the open casket and consoling the widow, he said, "I know this must be a very hard blow, Mrs. Vernon. But we must remember that what we see here is the husk only, the shell—the nut has gone to heaven."

—■—

A Church Garden
Three Rows of Squash
1. Squash indifference.
2. Squash criticism.
3. Squash gossip.

Four Rows of Turnips
1. Turn up for meetings.
2. Turn up with a smile.
3. Turn up with a visitor.
4. Turn up with a Bible.

Five Rows of Lettuce
1. Let us love one another.
2. Let us welcome strangers.
3. Let us be faithful to duty.
4. Let us truly worship God.
5. Let us give liberally.

—■—

GAS

Right in the middle of the service, and just before the sermon, a member of the congregation remembered she had forgotten to turn off the gas under the roast. Hurriedly she scribbled a note and passed it to the usher to give to her husband. Unfortunately, the usher misunderstood her intention and took it to the pulpit. Unfolding the note, the preacher read aloud, "Please go home and turn off the gas."

—■—

GIN

One priest to another, across the card table: "Forgive me, father, for I have ginned."

GIVING

A painter in California was asked to contribute to a drive being conducted by his church. "I'm broke," he explained, "but I'll contribute a $300 picture."

When the drive was completed, the minister explained that it was still $100 short of the goal. "OK," said the artist. "I'll increase the price of my picture to $400."

The doctor sent a note to his minister: "Sorry I haven't tithed for three months. But, you know, there's a lot of that going around.

A minister habitually told his congregation that if they needed a pastoral visit to drop a note in the offering plate. One evening after services he discovered a note that said: "I am one of your loneliest members and heaviest contributors. May I have a visit tomorrow evening?" It was signed by his wife.

God has given us two hands—one to receive with and the other to give with. We are not cisterns made for hoarding; we are channels made for sharing.

—Billy Graham

◼

A miser is a rich pauper.

◼

Someone asked, "What is the most sensitive nerve in the human body?"
The preacher answered, "The one that leads to the pocketbook."

◼

In the ruins of an old church, excavators found a queer-shaped basket filled with buttons. It must have been a collection plate.

—Judge

◼

When the usher came up the aisle with the basket at the offertory, a five-year-old boy in the pew in front turned to his father and said loudly and excitedly, "Daddy, here comes the pennyman!"

Mother: Quick, Henry, call the doctor. Johnny just swallowed a coin.

Father: I think we ought to send for the minister. He can get money out of anybody.

———◼———

One reason we have so many pennies in the church collection plate is because we have no smaller coin.

———◼———

When it comes to giving, some people stop at nothing.

———◼———

Three fellows went to church and when it came time to pass the plate, the three discovered they had no money. Not wanting to be embarrassed, one fainted and the other two carried him out.

———◼———

Some people who give the Lord credit are reluctant to give him cash.

—Jack Herbert

Minister before the morning offering: "The Lord owns the cattle on a thousand hills. He only needs cowboys to round them up. Will the ushers please come forward for the offering?"

■

Church Collection: a function in which many persons take only a passing interest.

■

GOD

He who leaves God out of his reckoning does not know how to count.

■

He who does not believe that God is above all is either a fool or has no experience of life.

—Caecilius Statius

■

Man: I will give you a candy bar if you will tell me where God is.

Boy: I will give you two candy bars if you will tell me where he is not.

GOLDEN RULE

"Always remember we are here to help others," said a mother as she explained the Golden Rule.

Her little one meditated for a moment and inquired, "Well, what are the others here for?"

◼

GOLF

A distinguished clergyman and one of his parishoners were playing golf. It was a very close match, and at the last hole the clergyman teed up, addressed the ball, and swung his driver with great force. The ball, instead of sailing down the fairway, merely rolled off the tee and settled slowly some twelve feet away.

The clergyman frowned, glared, and bit his lip, but said nothing. His opponent regarded him for a moment, and then remarked:

"Doctor, that is the most profane silence I have ever witnessed."

◼

Friend: Pastor, how do you let off steam when you miss a shot and your golf ball goes into a sand trap?

Pastor: I just repeat the names of some of the members of my congregation . . . with feeling!

GOOD

The man who says he is just as good as half the folks in the church seldom specifies which half.

— ■ —

GOOD FOR NOTHING

Two boys were trying to outdo each other. The first said, "My uncle's a doctor. I can be sick for nothing!" The second youngster shot back, "Big deal! My uncle is a preacher. I can be good for nothing!"

— ■ —

GOOD MEDICINE

Five-year-old Johnny was being urged by his mother to take some medicine.

"It's good for you, Johnny. And God wishes you to take it."

"I don't believe He does, Mother. I'll ask him." The youngster buried his head under the blankets on his bed and soon a hoarse voice came, "No, certainly not!"

— ■ —

GOODNESS

Sin writes histories; goodness is silent.

—Goethe

No hell will frighten men away from sin;
no dread of prospective misery; only
goodness can cast hell out of any man,
and set up the kingdom of heaven within.
—Hugh R. Haweis

GOOD SAMARITAN

Sunday school teacher: In the story of
the Good Samaritan, why did the Levite
pass by on the other side?

Student: Because the poor man had
already been robbed.

GOSSIP

"I think we need to change the morning
hymn," said the minister to his song
leader. "My topic this morning is 'gossip.' I
don't think 'I Love To Tell the Story' would
be the best song."

GRANDCHILDREN

God has many children, but no grand-
children.

GREAT

Great is the difference betwixt a man's being frightened at, and humbled for his sins.

—Thomas Fuller

GUARD

It is too late to be on our guard when we are in the midst of evils.

—Seneca

HALO

St. Peter's greeting as you approach the Gates: "Well, halo there!"

A halo has to fall only eleven inches to become a noose.

HAY

One Sunday as a farmer was getting in his hay crop his minister stopped by. The pastor asked the farmer if he had been to church. "To tell the truth, I would rather sit on the hay load and think about the church than sit in the church and think about hay."

HEADACHE

Little Susie, a six-year-old, complained, ''Mother, I've got a stomachache.''

''That's because your stomach is empty,'' the mother replied. ''You would feel better if you had something in it.''

That afternoon the minister called, and in conversation remarked he had been suffering all day with a severe headache.

Susie perked up. ''That's because it's empty,'' she said. ''You'd feel better if you had something in it.''

HEARING

The world is dying for want, not of good preaching, but of good hearing.

HEART

When God measures a man, He puts the tape around the heart instead of the head.

HEATHEN

After a special exhortation for support of foreign missions, the basket was passed. When it was presented to one man, he said to the holder of the basket, "I don't believe in missions."

"In that case," whispered the deacon, "take something out—it is for the heathen."

HEAVEN

To get to heaven, turn right and keep straight.

The distance from earth to heaven is not so much a matter of altitude as it is attitude.

Almost everybody is in favor of going to heaven, but too many people are hoping they'll live long enough to see an easing of the entrance requirements.

An exasperated mother, whose son was always getting into mischief, finally asked him, "How do you expect to get into heaven?"

The boy thought it over and said, "Well, I'll just run in and out and in and out and keep slamming the door until St. Peter says, 'For heaven's sake, Jimmy, come in or stay out.'"

A new group of male applicants had just arrived in heaven.

Peter looked them over and ordered, "All men who were henpecked on earth, please step to the left; all those who were bosses in their own homes, step to the right."

The line quickly formed on the left. Only one man stepped to the right.

Peter looked at the frail little man standing by himself and inquired, "What makes you think you belong on that side?"

Without hesitation, the meek little man explained, "Because this is where my wife told me to stand."

Heckler: Christianity hasn't done much good. It's been in the world for nineteen hundred years and look at the mess we're in.

Preacher: Soap has been in the world longer than that and look at the dirt on your face!

HELL

Hell is full of good meanings and wishings.

—Herbert

The man who tries to prove there is no hell, generally has a personal reason for doing so.

When a certain shameless fellow mockingly asked a pious old man what God had done before the creation of the world, the latter aptly countered that he had been building hell for the curious.

—John Clavin

The trouble about dying and going below is, when you get mad at your friends, where do you tell them to go?

■

A circuit rider, encountering many a meal that needed seasoning, carried with him a tiny bottle of tabasco sauce, and put it on the table before him at eating houses.

A stranger, eyeing it with curiosity, asked permission to try it. He put a liberal quantity on a piece of beef, which he then bolted. There was a pause.

The stranger (gulping down a glass of water)—"Say, parson, you preach hell, don't you?"

The circuit rider—"I feel it my duty to remind the wicked that there is retribution beyond the grave."

Stranger—"Anyhow, you're the first preacher I've seen that carries samples."

■

The only people I know who still believe in hell are the ones who had the proper kind of upbringing.

It doesn't matter what they preach,
  Of high or low degree;
The old hell of the Bible
  Is hell enough for me.

———◼———

The popular preacher, Charles Spurgeon, was admonishing a class of divinity students on the importance of making the facial expressions harmonize with the speech in delivering sermons. "When you speak of heaven," he said, "let your face light up and be irradiated with a heavenly gleam. Let your eyes shine with reflected glory. And when you speak of hell . . . well, then your everyday face will do."

———◼———

A very foul-mouthed man met the local pastor on the street one day and said, "Now, where in hell have I seen you?" To which the pastor replied, "From where in hell do you come, sir?"

———◼———

One gratifying impression we get from modern theological discussions is that hell is not as hot as it was forty years ago.
                                          —Toledo Blade

A motorist was picked up unconscious after a smash, and was being carried to a nearby filling station. Upon opening his eyes en route, he began to kick and struggle desperately to get away. Afterwards he explained that the first thing he saw was a "Shell" sign and somebody was standing in front of the "S"!

If there is no hell, a good many preachers are obtaining money under false pretenses.

—William A. Sunday

Hell is truth seen too late, duty neglected in its season.

The road to hell is paved with good intentions.

—Karl Marx

A woman dreamed that she was talking with her late husband. "Are you happy now?" she asked him.

"Very."

"Happier than you were on earth with me?"

"Yes."

"Tell me, darling, what's it like in heaven?"

"Who said I was in heaven?"

HOG CALLER

A local pastor joined a community service club and the members thought they would have some fun with him. Under his name on the badge they printed "Hog Caller" as his occupation.

Everyone made a big fanfare as the badge was presented. The pastor responded by saying: "I usually am called the 'Shepherd of the Sheep' . . . but you know your people better than I do."

HOMILY

Many a girl brought up on the Bible has become a homily woman.

HUMILITY

"Nothing sets a person so much out of the devil's reach as humility."

—Jonathan Edwards

———◼———

HYMN

What the world really needs is one more hymn: "I Did It Thy Way."

———◼———

A distinguished theologian was invited to address a Sunday school group. The divine spoke for over two hours and his remarks were of too deep a character for the average juvenile mind to comprehend. At the conclusion, the superintendent, according to custom, requested someone in the Sunday school to name an appropriate hymn to be sung.

"Sing 'Revive Us Again'," shouted a boy in the rear of the room.

———◼———

Three churches, all different denominations, were located on the same main intersection. One Sunday morning a passerby heard the first church singing, "Will There Be Any Stars in My Crown?"

The next church was singing, "No, Not One."

From the third church came, "Oh, That Will Be Glory For Me."

Instead of singing the Doxology phrase, "Praise all creatures here below," a little girl sang, "Praise all preachers, here we go." It made sense to her because everybody sang it at the end of the service, just as they were leaving.

━■━

A song leader had a very rough time when he was leading and didn't notice the words of the song. He said, "I want the women to sing the verse 'I will go home today,' and the men to come in on the chorus with 'Glad day, Glad day.'" The people were laughing too much to sing the song.

━■━

Q. What is the most appropriate of all songs for the choir to sing just after the morning sermon?

A. Awake, Ye Sinners.

HYPOCRITES

"I never go to church," boasted a wandering member. "Perhaps you have noticed that?"

"Yes, I have noticed that," said his pastor.

"Well, the reason I don't go is that there are so many hypocrites there."

"Oh, don't let that keep you away," replied the pastor, smiling blandly. "There is always room for one more, you know."

■

INCOME TAX

Did you hear about the man from the income tax bureau who phoned a certain Baptist minister to say, "We're checking the tax return of a member of your church, Deacon X., and notice he lists a donation to your building fund of three hundred dollars. Is that correct?" The minister answered without hesitation, "I haven't got my records available, but I'll promise you one thing: if he hasn't, he will!"

■

IMMERSE

Conversion by Baptist standards requires that you go from bad to immerse.

INFIDEL

An infidel sneered. "So many things in the world are made wrong. Look at that little acorn on that big tree and that big pumpkin on that little vine! People talk about an all-wise God at the head of this universe. Now if I had been doing it I would have put that acorn on the vine, and the pumpkin on the oak.

Just then an acorn fell and hit him on the head.

A listener was heard to remark, "What if it had been a pumpkin!"

INTERRUPT

Member to pastor at the end of the morning service: "Pastor, you were really good this morning! You interrupted my thoughts at least half a dozen times!"

ISAIAH

Question: Do you know what the name of Isaiah's horse was?

Answer: Is Me. He said, "Woe, is me."

JANITOR

Pastor: How do you like your job?

Janitor: It is a pushover. All I have to do is mind my keys and pews.

JOB

"Did you know that Job spoke when he was a very small baby?"

"Where does it say that?"

"It says 'Job cursed the day he was born.'"

Question: Why was Job always cold in bed?

Answer: Because he had such miserable comforters.

Q: Who was the most successful physician in the Bible?

A: Job; he had the most patience (patients).

JONAH

Question: How did the fish that swallowed Jonah obey the divine law?

Answer: Jonah was a stranger, and the fish took him in.

Question: Who was Jonah's tutor?
Answer: The fish that brought him up.

Q: How did Jonah feel when the great fish swallowed him?

A: Down in the mouth.

———■———

A lady turned to her young son and said, "Didn't you enjoy Mr. Wood's sermon about Jonah and the whale?"

"I guess so," the boy said. "But I feel just like that whale. All that preaching's given me a bellyache."

———■———

A guest on the speaker's platform was unexpectedly called upon to make a speech. He stammered for a moment, apologized for coming unprepared, then looked at the chairman and quoted Jonah's admonition to the whale:

"If you had kept your big mouth closed, I wouldn't be in this predicament now."

———■———

JOSEPH

Q: Who was the straightest man in the Bible?

A: Joseph. Pharaoh made a ruler out of him.

Q: What man in the Bible had no parents?

A: Joshua, the son of Nun.

JUDGE

A lady was showing a church friend her neighbor's wash through her back window. "Our neighbor isn't very clean. Look at those streaks on the wash!"

Replied her friend. "Those streaks aren't on your neighbor's wash. They're on your window."

JUDGMENT

It is a sin to believe evil of another, but it is seldom a mistake.

JUDGMENT DAY

"There will be thunder, lightning, floods, fires and earthquakes!" roared the preacher, describing Judgment Day.

Wide-eyed, a little boy in the congregation tugged at his mother's sleeve: "Will I get out of school?"

KING HEROD

During a seminary class, the lesson centered on the problem of King Herod offering up half his kingdom to see the daughter of Herodius dance.

"Now, what if you had this problem and you made the offer of anything she wanted and the girl came to you asking for the head of John the Baptist, and you didn't want to give her the head of John. What would you do?" asked the professor.

Soon a hand was raised, "I'd tell her," said one student, "that the head of John the Baptist was not in the half of the kingdom I was offering to her."

KNOCK KNOCK

Knock, knock.
Who's there?
Ach.
Ach who?
God bless you!

LANDLORD

A big, burly man called at the pastor's home and asked to see the minister's wife, a woman well known for her charitable impulses.

"Madam," he said in a broken voice, "I wish to draw your attention to the terrible plight of a poor family in this district. The father is dead, the mother is too ill to work, and the nine children are starving. They are about to be turned into the cold, cold streets unless someone pays their rent, which amounts to fifty dollars."

"How terrible!" exclaimed the lady, "May I ask who you are?"

The sympathetic visitor applied his handkerchief to his eyes. "I'm the landlord," he sobbed.

LAST WORDS

The seven last words of the church: WE NEVER DID IT THAT WAY BEFORE.

LATIN

Q: Name an outstanding feat of the Romans.

A: Speaking Latin.

LAYMAN

A layman is someone who lays in bed Sunday morning instead of going to church.

LIFESAVER

The sermons were always just twenty minutes in length. One day the preacher went one hour and twenty minutes. When asked why, he explained, "I always put a Lifesaver in my mouth and when it melts I know the twenty minutes are up. But in my hurry I put a button in my mouth by mistake!"

—■—

LIONIZE

Lionize . . . What the Romans did to the early Christians.

—■—

LITTLE

We can get too big for God, but we can't get too little.

—■—

LONG WINDED

The new preacher, at his first service, had a pitcher of water and a glass on the pulpit. As he preached, he drank until the pitcher of water was completely gone.

After the service someone asked an old woman of the church, "How did you like the new pastor?"

"Fine," she said, "but he's the first windmill I ever saw that was run by water."

LORD'S PRAYER

A small boy, repeating the Lord's Prayer one evening prayed:

"And forgive us our debts as we forgive those who are dead against us."

—■—

Children's versions of the Lord's Prayer:
—Our Father, Who are in heaven, hello! What be Thy name?
—Give us this day our daily breath
—Our Father, Who are in heaven, Hollywood be Thy name
—Our Father, Who art in heaven, Harold be Thy name
—Give us this day our jelly bread
—Lead us not into creation
—Deliver us from weevils—Deliver us from eagles

—■—

Two lawyers were bosom buddies. Much to the amazement of one, the other became a Sunday school teacher. "I bet you don't even know the Lord's Prayer," the first one fumed.

"Everybody knows that," the other replied. "It's 'Now I lay me down to sleep . . .'"

"You win," said the first one admiringly. "I didn't know you knew so much about the Bible."

LOT

Q: Why was the woman in the Bible turned into a pillar of salt?

A: Because she was dissatisfied with her Lot.

The Sunday school teacher was describing how Lot's wife looked back and suddenly turned into a pillar of salt.

"My mother looked back once while she was driving," contributed little Johnny, "and she turned into a telephone pole."

LOUDSPEAKER

In announcing the church's new public address system, the pastor told the congregation that the microphone and wiring had been paid for out of church funds. Then he added, "The loudspeaker has been donated by a member of the congregation in memory of his wife."

LYING

A minister wound up the services one morning by saying, "Next Sunday I am going to preach on the subject of liars. And in this connection, as a preparation for my discourse, I would like you all to read the 17th chapter of Mark." On the following Sunday, the preacher rose to begin, and said, "Now, then, all of you who have done as I requested and read the 17th chapter of Mark, please raise your hands." Nearly every hand in the congregation went up. Then said the preacher, "You are the people I want to talk to. There is no 17th chapter of Mark."

———◼———

MANSIONS

If you wish to dwell in the house of many mansions, you must make your reservation in advance.

———◼———

MARRIAGE

Man: Pastor, do you think it is right for one man to profit over another man's mistake?

Pastor: Why, most certainly not!

Man: Then would you mind returning the $25.00 I gave you last year for marrying me?

MARTIN LUTHER

A collector of rare books ran into an acquaintance of his who had just thrown away an old Bible that had been in his family for generations. He happened to mention that Guten something had printed it.

"Not Gutenberg?" gasped the book collector.

"Yes, that was the name."

"You idiot! You've thrown away one of the first books ever printed. A copy recently sold at an auction for $400,000."

"Mine wouldn't have been worth a dime," replied the man. "Some clown by the name of Martin Luther had scribbled all over it."

—■—

MATRIMONY

A minister forgot the name of a couple he was going to marry so he said from the pulpit, "Will those wishing to be united in holy matrimony please come forward after the service."

After the service thirteen old maids came forward.

MEMORY VERSE

Sunday school teacher: Do you remember your memory verse?

Student: I sure do. I even remember the zip code . . . John 3:16.

MEN'S FELLOWSHIP

A letter to the Men's Fellowship read, "All members are requested to bring their wives and one other covered dish to the annual banquet."

MILK AND HONEY

Sunday school teacher: What do you think the "land flowing with milk and honey" will be like?

Student: Sticky!

MINISTER

A minister was asked to inform a man with a heart condition that he had just inherited a million dollars. Everyone was afraid the shock would cause a heart attack and the man would die.

The minister went to the man's house and said, "Joe what would you do if you inherited a million dollars?" Joe responded, "Well, pastor, I think I would give half of it to the church."

And the minister fell over dead.

A tired minister was at home resting, and through the window he saw a woman approaching his door. She was one of those too-talkative people and he was not anxious to talk with her. He said to his wife: "I'll just duck upstairs and wait until she goes away."

An hour passed, then he tiptoed to the stair landing and listened. Not a sound. He was very pleased so he started down calling loudly to his wife, "Well, my dear, did you get rid of that old bore at last?"

The next moment he heard the voice of the same woman caller, and she couldn't possibly have missed hearing him. Two steps down, he saw them both staring up at him. It seemed truly a crisis moment.

The quick-thinking minister's wife answered, "Yes, dear, she went away over an hour ago. But Mrs. Jones has come to call in the meantime and I'm sure you'll be glad to greet her."

—■—

A clergyman had been invited to attend a party of the Sunday school nursery department. He decided to surprise them, so getting on his hands and knees, flapping his coattails over his head like wings, he hopped in on all fours cackling like a bird. Imagine his surprise when he learned that due to a switch in locations he had intruded on the ladies' missionary meeting!

— ∎ —

Member: How did you like the minister's sermon?

Friend: Well, frankly, I like our own minister better.

Member: Why is that?

Friend: It's the words they use. Our minister says, "In conclusion," and then he concludes. Your minister says, "Lastly," and he lasts.

— ∎ —

Q: Who can stay single even if he marries many women?

A: A minister.

— ∎ —

"How do you like the new minister?" a customer asked one of the merchants in town.

"I haven't heard him preach, but I like him fine," said the merchant.

"How can that be if you don't know him?"

"Oh, I can tell how good he is—the people are beginning to pay up their bills," said the merchant.

Delivering a speech at a banquet on the night of his arrival in a large city, a visiting minister told several anecdotes he expected to repeat at meetings the next day. Because he wanted to use the jokes again, he requested the reporters to omit them from any accounts they might turn in to their newspapers. A cub reporter, in commenting on the speech, ended his piece with the following: "The minister told a number of stories that cannot be published."

—■—

Ministers fall into four categories:

1. Those who do not have any notes and the people have no idea how long he will speak.
2. Those who put down on the podium in front of them each page of their sermon as they read it. These honest ones enable the audience to keep track of how much more is to come.
3. Those who cheat by putting each sheet of notes under the others in their hand.
4. And, worst of all, those who put down each sheet of notes as they read them and then horrify the audience by picking up the whole batch and reading off the other side.

While the minister was speaking, a man fell asleep. The minister raised his voice and pounded the pulpit but the man would not wake up. Finally, the minister called to a deacon, "Go wake that man up."

The deacon replied, "Wake him up yourself. You put him to sleep!"

—■—

"What is a prime minister?"

"A prime minister is a preacher at his best."

—■—

MINISTRY

Three preachers enjoyed a chicken dinner on the farm of a parishioner. After the meal the farmer took them around the yard. Seeing a rooster with its head lifted high, one minister remarked. "That fellow's pretty cocky, isn't he?"

The farmer's son who had been following them around exclaimed, "You'd be cocky too if you just had three sons enter the ministry!"

—■—

MIRACLE

A man asked the priest what a miracle was. A full explanation did not satisfy the man. "Now, won't Your Reverence give me an example of a miracle?"

"Well," said the priest, "step before me and I'll see what I can do." As the man did so, he gave him a terrific kick in the seat of his pants.

"Did you feel that?"

"I sure did feel it."

"Well," said the priest, "it would have been a miracle if you hadn't."

MISBEHAVE

After a spanking for being naughty, five-year-old Mark was advised to tell God that he was sorry. So at bedtime he folded his hands and explained to God that Satan had tempted him to misbehave. Then he turned to his mother and said, "God just told me he's going to spank Satan in the morning."

MODEL

The young preacher was flattered when someone described his as a "model" preacher.

His pride, however, soon vanished when he turned to his dictionary and found the definition of Model: "A small imitation of the real thing."

He was a little more cautious the next time. On being described as a "warm" preacher, he turned to his pocket dictionary, which read, "Warm . . . Not so hot."

MONKEY

I haven't much doubt that man sprang from the monkey, but where did the monkey spring from?

—Josh Billings

The Bible proves that men made monkeys of themselves, but science proves that monkeys made men of themselves.

MONEY

A Christian making money fast is just a man in a cloud of dust: it will fill his eyes if he be not careful.

—C. H. Spurgeon

If you want to know what God thinks of money, look at the people he gives it to.

MORAL COURAGE

A minister was speaking to a class of boys on the merits of moral courage. "Ten boys were sleeping in a dormitory," said he by way of illustration, "and only one knelt down to say his prayers. That is moral courage."

When he had finished his talk he asked one boy to give him an example of moral courage.

"Please, sir," said the lad, "ten ministers were sleeping in a dormitory and only one jumped into bed without saying his prayers."

MOSES

Teacher: You can be sure that if Moses were alive today, he'd be considered a remarkable man.

Lenny: He sure ought to be, he'd be more than 2,500 years old.

Question: Why was Moses the most wicked man who ever lived?

Answer: He broke the Ten Commandments all at once.

Father: What did you learn in Sunday school this morning?

Son: We learned about how Moses went behind enemy lines to rescue the Jews from the Egyptians. Moses ordered the engineers to build a pontoon bridge. After the people crossed, he sent bombers back to blow up the bridge and the Egyptian tanks that were following them. And then . . .

Father: Did your teacher really tell it like that?

Son: No, but if I told you what he said you would never believe it!

———◼———

Q: Where is medicine first mentioned in the Bible?

A: Where the Lord gives Moses two tablets.

———◼———

Q: Why did Moses cross the Red Sea?

A: To avoid Egyptian traffic.

———◼———

Teacher: Today I shall tell you a Bible story about Moses and the plagues sent on the people of Egypt. Does anyone know what a plague is?

Student: Yes, my brother is one.

NEW BIRTH

One excuse often used for not becoming a Christian is, "I don't understand the new birth." Of course, not many people understand love, but they get married anyway.

NOAH

As Noah remarked while the animals were boarding the Ark, "Now I herd everything."

A little boy, just back from Sunday school, asked his father if Noah had a wife.

"All the time, questions, questions, questions," replied the father. "Of course he did: Joan of Arc."

Question: How do we know that Noah had a pig in the Ark?

Answer: He had Ham.

Noah tried to teach the donkeys on the Ark to steer, but all they did was helm and haw.

Question: Where did Noah strike the first nail in the ark?

Answer: On the head.

———■———

Question: In what place did the cock crow when all the world could hear him?

Answer In Noah's Ark.

———■———

Question: What is the difference between Noah's Ark and an Archbishop?

Answer: One was a high ark, but the other is a hierarch.

———■———

Ned: What instructions did Noah give his sons about fishing off the Ark?

Fred: I don't know.

Ned: Go easy on the bait, boys. I have only two worms.

———■———

Q: Who was the best financier in the Bible?

A: Noah; he floated his stock while the whole world was in liquidation.

Q: Why didn't they play cards on Noah's Ark?
A: Because Noah sat on the deck.

━■━

Joe: Was there any money on Noah's Ark?"
Moe: Yes. The duck took a bill, the frog took a greenback, and the skunk took a scent.

━■━

One thing about Noah—he didn't miss the boat.

━■━

Teacher: Do you know who built the Ark?
Student: No.
Teacher: Correct.

━■━

Noah was standing at the gangplank checking off the pairs of animals when he saw three camels trying to get on board.
"Wait a minute!" said Noah. "Two each is the limit. One of you will have to stay behind."

"It won't be me," said the first camel. "I'm the camel whose back is broken by the last straw."

"I'm the one people swallow while straining at a gnat," said the second.

"I," said the third, "am the one that shall pass through the eye of a needle sooner than a rich man shall enter heaven."

"Come on in," said Noah, "the world is going to need all of you."

NODDING

"Did they like my sermon?" the anxious young minister asked his wife on their way home.

"I think so, dear," she replied, tactfully. "At least they were all nodding."

NOEL

A famous writer once sent Christmas cards containing nothing but twenty-five letters of the alphabet. When some of his friends admitted that they had failed to understand his message, he pointed to the card and cried, "Look! No 'L'!"

NOTES

A minister preached a very short sermon. He explained, "My dog got into my office and chewed up some of my notes."

At the close of the service a visitor asked, "If your dog ever has pups, please let my pastor have one of them."

NUDGE

The Christian's just desserts include nudge Sundays.

NURSERY

Sign of a church nursery: THEY SHALL NOT ALL SLEEP BUT THEY SHALL BE CHANGED.

NUTS TO YOU

A pastor got his note accompanying a box of goodies, addressed to him and his wife from an old lady in the parish:

"Dear Pastor: Knowing that you do not eat sweets, I am sending candy to your wife—and nuts to you."

OFFERING

An usher was passing the collection plate at a large church wedding. One of those attending looked up, very puzzled. Without waiting for the question, the usher nodded his head, "I know it's unusual; but the father of bride requested it."

■

Mother: Now remember to put some of your allowance in the offering at church.

Son: Why not buy an ice cream cone with it and let the cashier put it in the offering?

■

ORATORY

Church member: Pastor, you have a marvelous gift of oratory. How did you develop it?

Pastor: I learned to speak as men learn to skate or ride a bike . . . by doggedly making a fool of myself until I got used to it.

■

ORGANIST

The organist wanted to make an impression on the visiting clergyman with her musical accomplishment. She wrote a note to the old sexton who had been a little slack in his work of pumping enough air for the organ, and handed it to him just before the service started. But, making a natural mistake, the sexton passed the note on to the visiting clergyman, who opened it and read: "Keep blowing away until I give the signal to stop."

PASTOR

An elderly woman was weeping as she bade good-bye to the man who had been pastor of her church for several years.

"My dear lady," consoled the departing pastor, "don't get so upset. The bishop surely will send a much better pastor to replace me here."

"That's what they told us the last time," wailed the woman.

"The pastor teaches, though he must solicit his own classes. He heals, though without pills or knife. He is sometimes a lawyer, often a social worker, something of an editor, a bit of a philosopher and entertainer, a salesman, a decorative piece for public functions, and he is supposed to be a scholar. He visits the sick, marries people, buries the dead, labors to console those who sorrow and to admonish those who sin, and tries to stay sweet when chided for not doing his duty. He plans programs, appoints committees when he can get them, spends considerable time in keeping people out of each other's hair. Between times he prepares a sermon and preaches it on Sunday to those who don't happen to have any other engagement. Then on Monday he smiles when some jovial chap roars, "What a job—one day a week!"

◼

Clara: My pastor is so good he can talk on any subject for an hour.
Sarah: That's nothing! My pastor can talk for an hour without a subject!

◼

Did you hear about the young pastor who fouled up the established routine? He didn't stand at the door and shake hands with the worshipers after the service. He went out to the curb and shook hands with the red-faced parents waiting for their children to come out of Sunday school.

PATIENCE

Patience is the ability to stand something as long as it happens to the other fellow.

PERFECT

Preacher: Does anyone know anyone who is perfect?

A little man in the back of the church raised his hand.

Preacher: Who do you know that is perfect?

Little man: My wife's first husband.

PEST

Wife: Who was that at the door, dear?

Husband: It was that new minister. He has been by four times this week.

Wife: What is his name?

Husband: I think it's Pester Smith.

PIANO PLAYER

A circuit preacher rode into a backwoods town and set up a series of camp meetings. The first evening he asked for a volunteer piano player so the congregation could sing. He promptly got a volunteer and the hymnals were distributed.

"All right," said the preacher. "Let's all sing hymn number 4."

"Sorry, preacher," said the piano player. "I don't know hymn number 4."

"That's OK," said the enthusiastic preacher. "We'll just sing hymn number 27. Everybody knows it."

The piano player squirmed a bit on his bench and said, "Sorry preacher, I don't know hymn number 27."

The preacher, keeping his good nature, said, "Don't feel badly about it. We'll just sing hymn number 34. Everybody learned that when they were small children."

The piano player was really nervous by now and said, "Sorry preacher, but I guess I don't know hymn number 34.

Whereupon someone in the back shouted, "That piano player is an idiot!"

"Hold it!" exclaimed the preacher. "I want that man who called the piano player an idiot to stand up."

No one stood.

"If he won't stand up, I want the man sitting beside the man who called the piano player an idiot to stand up."

No one stood.

After a brief period of complete silence, a little fellow in the back stood up and said, "Preacher, I didn't call the piano player an idiot, and I'm not sitting beside the man who called the piano player an idiot . . . what I want to know, is who called that idiot a piano player?"

PIOUS

A profoundly pious look will not cover a poorly prepared message.

PHOENICIANS

Sunday school teacher: What were the Phoenicians famous for?
Student: Blinds.

PLEDGES

The deacon ran into the pastor's office and exclaimed excitedly, "Pastor, I have terrible news to report! Burglars must've broken in last night . . . they stole ninety thousand dollars worth of pledges!"

PRACTICE

"I can't go around practicing what I preach. I'd work myself to death."

You know what's wrong with religion today? There are too many people practicing it—and not enough people good at it!

— ■ —

PRAISE

"The pastor will be gone tonight, and we will be having a service of singing and praise."

— ■ —

PRAISE THE LORD

Did you hear about the country parson who decided to buy himself a horse? The dealer assured him that the one he selected was a perfect choice. "This here horse," he said, "has lived all his life in a religious atmosphere. So remember that he'll never start if you order 'Giddyap.' You've got to say, 'Praise the Lord.' Likewise, a 'Whoa' will never make him stop. You've got to say, 'Amen.' "

Thus forewarned, the parson paid for the horse, mounted him and with a cheery "Praise the Lord" sent him wandering off in the direction of the parson's parish. Suddenly, however, he noticed that the road ahead had been washed out, leaving a chasm two hundred yards deep. In a panic, he forgot his instructions and cried "Whoa" in vain several times. The horse just cantered on. At the very last moment he remembered to cry "Amen" . . . and the horse stopped short at the very brink of the chasm. But alas! That's when the parson, out of force of habit, murmured fervently, "Praise the Lord!"

PRAYER

I don't believe in all this popularizing of religion. Somehow I can't ever see myself saying, "Our Dad who art in heaven.

"Dear God, we had a good time at church today. I wish you could have been there."

If prayers were puddings, many men would starve.

Sunday school teacher: What is prayer?

Student: That is a message sent to God at night and on Sundays when the rates are lower.

A bedtime prayer that was overheard: "I'm not praying for anything for myself . . . just a new bike for my brother that we can both ride."

———————

Many a man who prays on his knees on Sunday, preys on his friends the rest of the week.

———————

Little Billy was kneeling beside his bed and prayed, "Dear God, if You can find some way to put the vitamins in candy and ice cream instead of in spinach and cod liver oil, I would sure appreciate it. Amen."

———————

Little Mary, the daughter of a radio announcer, was invited to a friend's house for dinner. The hostess asked if Mary would honor them by saying grace.

Delighted, the little girl cleared her throat, looked at her wrist watch and said, "This food, friends, is coming to you through the courtesy of Almighty God!"

A hungry little boy was beginning to eat his dinner when his father reminded him that they hadn't prayed.

"We don't have to," said the little boy. "Mommy is a good cook!"

—■—

Little Susie concluded her prayer by saying: "Dear God, before I finish please take care of Daddy, Mommy, my baby brother, Grandma, and Grandpa . . . and please, God, take care of yourself, or else we're all sunk!"

—■—

The pastor visited the Sunday evening youth group and volunteers were called on to pray. A little girl volunteered to pray for the pastor. Her prayer: "Be with our pastor and help him to preach a better sermon next Sunday."

—■—

After a family disturbance one of the little boys closed his bedtime prayer by saying, "And please don't give my dad any more children . . . He don't know how to treat those he's got now."

The teacher handed out the test papers and told the children they could start answering the questions.

She noticed little Billy sitting with his head bowed, his hands over his face. She approached him.

"Don't you feel well?" she inquired.

"Oh, I'm fine, teacher. Maybe it's unconstitutional, but I always pray before a test!"

—■—

So this big-wheel Russian is riding along when he sees a peasant, kneeling in the middle of a field, praying. He stops the car, stomps over and says:

"Aha! You waste your time like this instead of plowing and planting for the Party!"

"But, Commissar, I'm praying for the Party!"

"Praying for the Party! Huh! And years ago, you probably prayed for the Czar!"

"I did, Commissar."

"Well . . . look what happened to him!"

"Right!"

Little Timmy was saying his prayers one night. His mother overheard this entreaty: "And please make Tommy stop throwing things at me. By the way, I've mentioned this before."

Billy: What are prayers anyway?
Mother: They are messages sent to Heaven.
Billy: Well . . . do I pray at night because the rates are cheaper?

—■—

After attending a prayer meeting where everyone prayed very loud, a little boy remarked, "If they lived nearer to God they wouldn't have to pray so loud."

—■—

Little Jane, whose grandmother was visiting her family, was going to bed when her mother called:
"Don't forget, dear, to include Grandma in your prayers tonight, that God should bless her and let her live to be very, very old."
"Oh, she's old enough," replied Jane. "I'd rather pray that God would make her young."

Little Dennis began falling out of a tree and cried, "Lord, save me, save me!" There was a pause and then he said, "Never mind, Lord, my pants just caught on a branch."

—◼︎—

The pastor was invited over for dinner and asked to lead in prayer for the meal. After the brief prayer, Junior said approvingly, "You don't pray so long when you're hungry, do you?"

—◼︎—

Mother: That's no way to say your prayers.

Daughter: But Mom, I thought that God was tired of hearing the same old stuff every night . . . so I told Him the story of the Three Bears instead.

—◼︎—

The fewer words the better the prayer.
—Martin Luther

One friend to another, "You drive the car and I'll pray."

"What's the matter; don't you trust my driving?"

"Don't you trust my praying?"

———■———

Nowadays the only time people seem to get on their knees is when looking for a contact lens.

———■———

An ocean liner was sinking and the captain yelled: "Does anybody know how to pray?"

A minister on board said, "I do."

"Good," said the captain. "You start praying. The rest of us will put on the life belts. We are one belt short."

———■———

PREACH

The parson of a tiny congregation in Arkansas disappeared one night with the entire church treasury, and the local constable set out to capture him. This he did, dragging the culprit back by the collar a week later. "Here's the varmit, folks," announced the constable grimly. "I'm sorry to say he has already squandered our money, but I drug him back so we can make him preach it out."

PREACHER

One young preacher made a mistake when he encouraged his listeners to be filled with fresh veal and new zigor.

The test of a preacher is that his congregation goes away saying not, "What a lovely sermon" but, "I will do something!"
—St. Francis de Sales

A little boy in church, awaking after a nap, asked his father. "Has the preacher finished?"

"Yes, son, he has finished, but he hasn't stopped."

Dwight L. Moody, the famous evangelist, stopped to visit with a fellow clergyman. The friend told Moody he would love to have him address his congregation, but that it would probably be embarrassing since the congregation was in the habit of walking out before a sermon was finished—no matter who the preacher was.

Moody said he would be delighted to take his chances and thought he would be able to hold them there until the end.

On Sunday morning Moody mounted the pulpit and began by pointing out that the first half of his sermon would be addressed to the sinners and the last half to the saints in the congregation. All stayed to the end.

■

A preacher was called upon to substitute for the regular minister, who had failed to reach the church because he was delayed in a snowstorm. The speaker began by explaining the meaning of a substitute. "If you break a window," he said, "and then place a cardboard there instead, that is a substitute."

After the sermon, a woman who had listened intently shook hands with him, and wishing to compliment him, said, "You were no substitute . . . you were a real pane!"

■

Preacher: "Please take it easy on the bill for repairing my car. Remember, I am a poor preacher."

Mechanic: "I know; I heard you Sunday!"

After returning from church one Sunday a small boy said, "You know what, Mommy, I'm going to be a minister when I grow up."

"That's fine," said his mother. "But what made you decide you want to be a preacher?"

"Well," said the boy pensively, "I'll have to go to church on Sunday anyway, and I think it would be more fun to stand up and yell than to sit still and listen."

IDEAL PREACHER

He preaches exactly 20 minutes and then sits down. He condemns sin, but never hurts anyone's feelings. He works from 8:00 a.m. to 10:00 p.m. in every type of work, from preaching to taxi service. He makes $60.00 a week, wears good clothes, buys good books regularly, has a nice family, drives a good car and gives $30.00 a week to the church. He also stands ready to contribute to every good work that comes along. He is 26 years old and has been preaching for 30 years. He is tall and short, thin and heavyset, plain-looking but handsome. He has one brown eye and one blue, hair parted in the middle, left side straight and dark, the other side wavy and blonde. He has a burning desire to work with teenagers, and spends all his time with the older folks. He smiles all the time with a straight face, because he has a sense of humor that keeps him seriously dedicated to his work.

He makes 15 calls a day on church members, spends all his time evangelizing the unchurched and is never out of his office. He is truly a remarkable person . . . and he does not exist.

—■—

PREACHING

One Sunday a farmer went to church. When he entered he saw that he and the preacher were the only ones present. The preacher asked the farmer if he wanted him to go ahead and preach. The farmer said, "I'm not too smart, but if I want to feed my cattle and only one showed up, I'd feed him." So the minister began his sermon.

One hour passed, then two hours, then two-and-a-half hours. The preacher finally finished and came down to ask the farmer how he had liked the sermon.

The farmer answered slowly, "Well, I'm not very smart, but if I went to feed my cattle and only one showed up, I sure wouldn't feed him all the hay."

1st Preacher: I think a pastor needs to study diligently for his Sunday morning message.

2nd Preacher: I disagree. Many times I have no idea what I am going to preach about but I go into the pulpit and preach and think nothing of it.

1st Preacher: And you are quite right in thinking nothing of it. Your deacons have told me they share your opinion.

PROCRASTINATION

After hearing his dad preach on "Justification," "Sanctification," and all the other "ations," a minister's son was ready when his Sunday school teacher asked if anybody knew what "procrastination" meant. "I'm not sure what it means," he said, "but I know our church believes in it."

PRODIGAL SON

A little boy told the story of the Prodigal Son for his Sunday school class:

"He sold his coat to buy food.

He sold his shirt to buy food.

He sold his undershirt to buy food, and then he came to himself."

Teacher: Who was sorry when the Prodigal Son returned home.
Student: The fatted calf.

———◼———

MELODY IN F
(THE PRODIGAL SON)

Feeling footloose and frisky, a feather-
brained fellow
Forced his fond father to fork over the
farthings.
And flew far to foreign fields
And frittered his fortune feasting
fabulously with faithless friends.
Fleeced by his fellows in folly, and facing
famine,
He found himself a feed-flinger in a filthy
farm yard.
Fairly famishing, he fain would have filled
his frame
With foraged food from fodder
fragments.
"Fooey, my father's flunkies fare far
finer,"
The frazzled fugitive forlornly fumbled,
frankly facing facts.
Frustrated by failure, and filled with
foreboding,
He fled forthwith to his family.
Falling at his father's feet, he forlornly
fumbled

"Father, I've flunked,
And fruitlessly forfeited family fellowship
  favor."
The far-sighted father, forestalling further
  flinching,
Frantically flagged the flunkies to
Fetch a fatling from the flack and fix a
  feast.
The fugitive's fault-finding brother
  frowned
On fickle forgiveness of former folderol.
But the faithful father figured,
"Filial fidelity is fine, but the fugitive is
  found!
What forbids fervent festivity?
Let flags be unfurled! Let fanfares flare!"
Father's forgiveness formed the foun-
  dation
For the former fugitive's future fortitude!

—◼—

PROMISE

Two sailors were adrift on a raft in the
ocean. They had just about given up hope
of rescue. One began to pray, "O Lord,
I've led a worthless life. I've been unkind
to my wife and I've neglected my children,
but if you'll save me, I promise . . ."

The other shouted. "Hold it. I think I see
land."

PROVERB

Proverb: a short sentence based on long experience.

Proverbs: the wisdom of many and the wit of one.

PUBLICAN

The seventh grade lesson dealt with the publican and the sinner. Asked the teacher, "What is a publican?"

Answered one of his wiser students: "The opposite of a democrat."

POLYGAMY

A Mormon acquaintance once pushed Mark Twain into an argument on the issue of polygamy. After long and tedious expositions justifying the practice, the Mormon demanded that Twain cite any passage of scripture expressly forbidding polygamy.

"Nothing easier," Twain replied. 'No man can serve two masters.' "

PUSH

A Baptist minister rushed down to the train station every single day to watch the Sunset Limited go by. There was no chore he wouldn't interrupt to carry out his ritual. Members of his congregation deemed his eccentricity juvenile and frivolous, and asked him to give it up. "No, gentlemen," he said firmly. "I preach your sermons, teach your Sunday school, bury your dead, marry you, run your charities, chairman every drive it pleases you to conduct. I won't give up seeing that Southern Pacific train every day. I love it! It's the only thing in this town I don't have to push!"

QUAKER

A Quaker became exasperated with his cow for kicking over a pail of milk.

He warned, "Thou knowest that, because of my religion, I can't punish thee. But if thee doeth that again, I will sell thee to a Baptist preacher and he will kick thee so thee won't be able to kick it over again!"

A minister who paid more attention to the pleasures of life than to his sermons was taken to task for his worldliness by his Quaker friend. The rebuke he received was tactful. "Friend," said the Quaker, "I understand thee's clever at fox-catching."

"I have few equals and no superiors at that sport," the minister replied complacently.

"Nevertheless, friend," said the Quaker, "if I were a fox I would hide where thee never would find me."

"Where would you hide?" asked the minister with a frown.

"Friend, I would hide in thy study."

RADIO

Radio prayer: "Lord, comfort those who are afflicted by the radio today."

REAPING

The chaplain was passing through the prison garment factory. "Sewing?" he said to a prisoner who was at work. "No, chaplain," replied the prisoner gloomily, "reaping!"

RELIGION

Still religion, like still water, is the first to freeze.

—

Many people treat their religion as a spare tire—they never use it except in an emergency.

—

It is the test of a good religion whether you can joke about it.

—Gilbert K. Chesterton

—

Religion is the best armor in the world, but the worst cloak.

—Bunyan

—

REPEATING

The new minister stood at the church door greeting parishioners as they departed after the close of services. The people were generous in complimenting the clergyman for his sermon, except one fellow who said to him, "Pretty dull sermon, Reverend." And in a minute or two the same man appeared again on line and said, "Pretty dull sermon, Reverend." Once again the man appeared, this time muttering, "You really didn't say anything at all, Reverend."

When he got the opportunity, the minister pointed out the triple-threat pest to one of the deacons and inquired about him. "Oh, don't let that guy bother you," said the deacon. "He's a poor soul who goes around repeating whatever he hears other people saying."

REPUTATION

A reputation once broken may possibly be repaired, but the world will always keep their eyes on the spot where the crack was.

—Joseph Hall

RICH

It's hard for a rich man to enter the kingdom of heaven, but it's easy for him to get on the church board of trustees.

RIDDLE

Q: Who is the smallest man in the Bible?

A: Some people believe that it was Zacchaeus. Others believe it was Nehemiah (Ne-high-a-miah), or Bildad, the Shuhite. But in reality it was Peter, the disciple—he slept on his watch!

—■—

Question: Where was deviled ham mentioned in the Bible?

Answer: When the evil spirits entered the swine.

—■—

Q: When is high finance first mentioned in the Bible?

A: When Pharaoh's daughter took a little prophet (profit) from the bulrushes.

—■—

Q: Who was the most popular actor in the Bible?

A: Samson. He brought the house down.

—■—

Q: Who was Round John Virgin?

A: One of the twelve opossums.

Q: When did Moses sleep with five people in one bed?
A: When he slept with his forefathers.

———■———

Teacher: Where was Solomon's temple?
Student: On the side of his head.

———■———

Q: When was money first mentioned in the Bible?
A: When the dove brought the green back to the ark.

———■———

Q: Why are there so few men with whiskers in heaven?
A: Because most men get in by a close shave.

———■———

Q: How were the Egyptians paid for goods taken by the Israelites when they fled from Egypt?
A: The Egyptians got a check on the bank of the Red Sea.

Q: How do we know they used arithmetic in early Bible times?

A: Because the Lord said to multiply on the face of the earth.

———■———

Q: Why didn't the last dove return to the Ark?

A: Because she had sufficient grounds to stay away.

———■———

Q: Who sounded the first bell in the Bible?

A: Cain, when he hit Abel.

———■———

RUTH

Question: When did Ruth treat Boaz badly?

Answer: When she pulled his ears and trod on his corn.

———■———

SACRED

The minister's new secretary, a former worker in the Pentagon, was busily reorganizing her boss's filing system. She labeled one drawer ''Sacred'' and the other ''Top Sacred.''

SALARY

The three sons of a lawyer, a doctor, and a minister, respectively, were talking about how much money their fathers made.

The lawyer's son said, "My father goes into court on a case and often comes home with as much as fifteen hundred dollars."

The doctor's son said, "My father performs an operation and earns as much as two thousand dollars for it."

The minister's son, determined not to be outdone, said, "That's nothing. My father preaches for just twenty minutes on Sunday morning and it takes four men to carry the money."

———◼———

Friend: Say, Pastor, how is it that you're so thin and gaunt while your horse is so fat and sleek?

Pastor: Because I feed the horse and the congregation feeds me.

———◼———

SAMSON

Q: What simple affliction brought about the death of Samson?

A: Fallen arches.

A Sunday school teacher asked her class to write a composition on the story of Samson. One teen-age girl wrote, "Samson wasn't so unusual. The boys I know brag about their strength and wear their hair long too."

SARCASM
Sarcasm is the language of the devil.

SATAN
Beware of Satan or evil have his way.

Satan as a master is bad, his work worse, his wages worst of all.

Satan keeps school for neglected children.

SEMINARY
Seminary . . . A place where they bury the dead.

SERMON

The sermon you enjoy most is not likely to be the one that will do you the most good.

—■—

Willie got very tired of the long sermon at church.

"If we give him the money now, ma, will he let us go out?" he asked in a loud whisper.

—■—

Sermons are like babies: easy to conceive . . . hard to deliver.

—■—

Pastor: How did the assistant pastor do Sunday morning?

Member: It was a poor sermon. Nothing in it at all.

(Upon seeing the assistant pastor, the following conversation took place)

Pastor: How did it go Sunday morning?

Assistant: Excellent. I didn't have time to prepare anything myself, so I preached on of your sermons.

An old farmer came back from church where he had gone alone.

"Was the sermon good?" inquired his wife.

"Yes."

"What was it about?" persisted his wife.

"Sin."

"Well, what did he say?"

"He was against it."

■

Student: Does a good beginning and a good ending make a good sermon?

Professor: If they're close enough together.

■

1st Member: I thought the sermon was divine. It reminded me of the peace of God. It passed all understanding.

2nd Member: I thought it reminded me of the mercies of God. I thought it would endure forever.

A new preacher had just begun his sermon. He was a little nervous and about ten minutes into the talk his mind went blank. He remembered what they had taught him in seminary when a situation like this would arise—repeat your last point. Often this would help you remember what is coming next. So he thought he would give it a try.

"Behold, I come quickly," he said. Still his mind was blank. He thought he would try it again. "Behold I come quickly." Still nothing.

He tried it one more time with such force he fell forward, knocking the pulpit to one side, tripping over a flower pot and falling into the lap of a little old lady in the front row.

The young preacher apologized and tried to explain what happened. "That's all right, young man," said the little old lady. "It was my fault. I should have gotten out of the way. You told me three times you were coming!"

—■—

The average man's idea of a good sermon is one that goes over his head—and hits one of his neighbors.

One beautiful Sunday morning, a minister announced to his congregation: "My good people, I have here in my hands three sermons—a $100 sermon that lasts five minutes, a $50 sermon that lasts fifteen minutes and a $10 sermon that lasts a full hour. Now, we'll take the collection and see which one I'll deliver."

A young preacher who lost his Sunday morning sermon notes said to the audience that he would have to depend on the Lord for the message. He went on to inform the people that if they would come back in the evening he would be better prepared.

A sermon's length is not its strength.

Member: Pastor, how did you get that cut on your face?

Pastor: I was thinking about my sermon this morning and wasn't concentrating on what I was doing and cut myself while shaving.

Member: That's too bad! Next time you had better concentrate on your shaving and cut your sermon!

Because of the overflow on a Sunday morning, a pastor was forced to hold two identical morning services. One Sunday he noticed a member arrive very late during the nine-thirty service. To his surprise, the member was in his seat when the eleven o'clock service began. But when the congregation rose to sing the hymn before the sermon, he left, explaining to the usher, "This is where I came in."

—■—

Rocking horse sermon—back and forth, back and forth, but going nowhere.

Mockingbird sermon—repetition, nothing new.

Smorgasbord sermon—a little bit of everything, but nothing solid.

Jericho sermon—march around the subject seven times.

Christmas tree sermon—something offered for nothing.

—■—

SHADOW

Sin and her shadow, death.

—Milton

SICK WOMAN

The minister's little daughter was sent to bed with a stomachache and missed her usual romp with her daddy. A few minutes later she appeared at the top of the stairs and called to her mother, "Mama, let me talk with Daddy."

"No, my dear, not tonight. Get back in bed."

"Please, mama."

"I said 'no.' That's enough now."

"Mother, I'm a very sick woman, and I must see my pastor at once."

—■—

SIN

Only the wages of sin have no deductions.

—■—

How candid we are in confessing other people's sin.

—■—

A Sunday school teacher asked a little girl: "What are the sins of omission?"

After some thought, she answered: "They're the sins we ought to have committed but haven't."

A minister told his congregation that there were 739 different sins. He already has received 73 requests for the list.

——■——

A nice but blundering old lady liked the new pastor and wanted to compliment him as she was leaving church after services. So she said to him, "I must say, sir, that we folks didn't know what sin was until you took charge of our parish."

——■——

Teacher: What must we do before we can receive the forgiveness of sins?
Student: We must sin.

——■——

"Many people develop a split personality because they try to be a sinner and a saint at the same time."
—Herbert A. Streeter

——■——

There is no "original sin." No matter how unusual it is, it has been thought of before by thousands.
—St. Louis Daily Globe-Democrat

SKATES

Q: Why is a pair of skates like the forbidden fruit in the Garden of Eden?

A: Both come before the fall.

———◼———

SLEEP

"How late do you usually sleep on Sunday morning?"

"It all depends."

"Depends on what?"

"The length of the sermon."

———◼———

Jack: Do you know Pete Wilson?

Mack: I sure do. We slept in the same church pew for over fifteen years.

———◼———

As they were leaving church one Sunday, a man confided to his friend he was suffering from insomnia. The friend asserted he had no trouble getting to sleep.

"Really?" he inquired. "Do you count sheep?"

"No," was the retort, "I talk to the shepherd."

A parishioner had dozed off to sleep during the morning service.

"Will all who want to go to heaven stand?" the preacher asked.

All stood, except the sleeping parishioner.

After they sat down, the pastor continued: "Well, will all who want to go to the other place stand?"

Someone suddenly dropped a songbook and the sleeping man jumped to his feet and stood sheepishly facing the preacher. "I don't know what we're voting for, but it looks like you and I are the only ones for it."

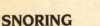

SMALLER

The smaller we are the more room we have for God.

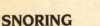

SNORING

"Did you hear Robinson snoring in church this morning? It was simply awful."

"Yes, I did—he woke me up."

SODOM & GOMORRAH

God's destruction of the wicked cities of Sodom and Gomorrah is another story that makes a vivid impression. A teacher relating the story to her class was saying, "Lot was warned to take his wife and flee out of the city which was about to be destroyed. Lot got away safely. His wife looked back and was turned to a pillar of salt. Now, children, do you have any questions to ask about this story?"

A boy raised his hand. "Could you please tell us what happened to the flea?"

———

Sunday school teacher: What was Dan and Beersheba?

Pupil: I think they were husband and wife almost like Sodom and Gomorrah.

———

SOLOMON

"King Solomon," declared a little girl in Sunday school, "is my favorite character in the Bible—because he was so kind to ladies and animals." The startled teacher demanded, "Who told you that?" "Nobody told me; I read it myself in the Bible," asserted the little girl. "It says Solomon kept seven hundred wives and three hundred porcupines."

Rich: Why was Solomon the wisest man in the world?

Dave: Because he had so many wives to advise him.

—■—

SOUND

A husband, unable to attend church on a Sunday morning when the preacher was candidating for the pulpit asked his wife, Was he sound?"

Her reply, "He was all sound!"

—■—

SPANK

After spanking, a father returned to his son's room to encourage and admonish him. "I really didn't want to spank you, but the Bible says that children should obey their parents."

"I know," was the tearful reply. "But the Bible also says, 'Be ye kind one to another,' too."

—■—

STAINED GLASS

A three-year-old boy gazed in delight at the handsome stained glass windows in a church, and told his mother, "Look—cartoons!"

STRAIGHT AND NARROW

"The dull thing about going the straight and narrow path is that you so seldom meet anybody you know."

STUMBLING BLOCK

You can't build a church with stumbling blocks.

ST. PETER

St. Peter looked at the new arrival skeptically; he had no advance knowledge of his coming.

"How did you get there?" he asked.

"Flu."

SUNDAY

An elderly lady, when asked to give her opinion of her pastor, said that on six days a week he was invisible, and on the seventh he was incomprehensible.

If all the autos in the world were laid end to end, it would be Sunday afternoon.

Question: What is the strongest day in the week?

Answer: Sunday. The rest are weekdays.

If people would quit digging pits on Saturday night, there wouldn't be so many oxen in the ditch on Sunday morning.

Little Raymond came home beaming from church. He rushed up the stairs and yelled, "Mommy, Mommy, Father Alonzo said something awfully nice about me in his prayer this morning. He said 'O Lord, we thank Thee for our food and Raymond.'"

The Sunday school teacher had just concluded a talk on the creation account as given in Genesis, when one of the children said, "My father says we are descended from monkeys."

"After class," replied the teacher, "we will discuss your private family problems."

"Mommy," said little Judy, "did you ever see a cross-eyed bear?"

"Why, no, Judy" chuckled her mother, "but why do you ask?"

"Well, in Sunday school this morning, we sang about 'the consecrated cross-eyed bear.' "

A Sunday school teacher asked a little girl if she said her prayers every night.

"No, not every night," declared the child. " 'Cause some nights I don't want anything!"

A little boy forgot his lines in a Sunday school presentation. His mother was in the front row to prompt him. She gestured and formed the words silently with her lips, but it did not help. Her son's memory was blank.

Finally, she leaned forward and whispered the cue, "I am the light of the world."

The child beamed and with great feeling and a loud clear voice said, "My mother is the light of the world."

Teacher: Why did Jesus know the Scriptures so well?

Student: Oh, that's easy. His Daddy wrote them.

———■———

Teacher: Who were the twin boys in the Bible?

Student: That's easy, First and Second Samuel!

———■———

Teacher: What parable in the Bible do you like best?

Student: The one about the fellow that loafs and fishes.

———■———

"Daddy, I want to ask you a question," said little Bobby after his first day in Sunday school.

"Yes, Bobby, what is it?"

"The teacher was reading the Bible to us—all about the children of Israel building the temple, the children of Israel crossing the Red Sea, the children of Israel making sacrifices. Didn't the grownups do anything?"

Overheard after Sunday school:

"Is it true that shepherds have dirty socks?"

"What do you mean?"

"I heard that the shepherds washed their socks by night.

A little boy was writing the memory verse for the day on the blackboard: "DO ONE TO OTHERS AS OTHERS DO ONE TO YOU."

A little boy came home from Sunday school and told his mother that they had just learned a new song about a boy named Andy. His mother couldn't understand what he meant until he sang:

"Andy walks with me,
Andy talks with me,
Andy tells me I am his own . . ."

Sunday school teacher: And where can you find the Beatitudes?

Pupil: Have you tried the Yellow Pages?

Son: Dad, did you go to Sunday school when you were young?

Dad: Never missed a Sunday.

Son: Bet it won't do me any good either.

—■—

Sunday school teacher: Why do you believe in God?

Small Student: I guess it just runs in our family.

—■—

A Sunday school teacher asked her students to draw a picture of the Holy Family. After the pictures were brought to her, she saw that some of the youngsters had drawn the conventional pictures—the Holy Family and the manger, the Holy Family riding on the mule, etc.

But she called up one little boy to ask him to explain his drawing, which showed an airplane with four heads sticking out of the plane windows.

She said, "I can understand you drew three of the heads to show Joseph, Mary and Jesus. But who's the fourth head?"

"Oh," answered the boy, "that's Pontius the pilot!"

Teacher: Johnny, you should't talk so loudly in Sunday school.

Johnny: Billy Graham does.

———■———

Sunday school teacher: Why would it be wrong to cut off a cat's tail?

Student: The Bible says, "What God has joined together, let no man put asunder.."

———■———

"I cried at Sunday school," the boy reported to his mother after surviving his first session.

"Why did you cry?"

"I looked around the room, and I was the only guy there that I knew!

———■———

There was, for example, the six-year-old boy who wrote, "My favorite Bible story is the one where the plowshares are turned into Fords."

———■———

Question: What does the story of Jonah and the great fish teach us?

Answer: You can't keep a good man down.

Question: Which came first, the chicken or the egg?

Answer: The chicken, of course. God couldn't lay an egg.

TEMPER

"That's what I like about you . . . when your golf ball goes into the rough, you don't swear."

"That may be . . . but where I spit, the grass dies!"

TEMPTATION

"Opportunity knocks only once," one preacher warned his flock, "but temptation bangs on your door for years."

The road to success is dotted with many tempting parking places.

When you flee temptation, be sure you don't leave a forwarding address.

TENNIS

Q: Where is tennis mentioned in the Bible?

A: When Joseph served in Pharaoh's court.

—■—

TEN COMMANDMENTS

If God had believed in permissiveness, He would have given us the Ten Suggestions.

—■—

As Moses said to the multitude when he showed them the Ten Commandments, "You might say they're nonnegotiable demands."

—■—

When a Sunday school class was asked to write out the Ten Commandments, one boy put down for the fifth, "Humor thy father and thy mother."

TESTIMONY

Testimony is like an arrow shot from a long bow; the force of it depends on the strength of the hand that draws it. Argument is like an arrow from a cross-bow, which had equal force though shot by a child.

TOASTMASTER

Member: Pastor, a friend of mine died and I would like you to act as master of ceremonies at his burial service.

Pastor: Where is he going to be buried?

Member: Oh, he is going to be cremated.

Pastor: You don't want a master of ceremonies. What you need is a toastmaster.

TONGUE

Once when C. H. Spurgeon, then a young man, was passing by the house of a woman with a poison tongue, she let him have a volley of impolite words. "Yes, thank you; I am quite well," Spurgeon said. Then she let out another volley. "Yes, it does look as if it's going to rain," he replied. Surprised, the woman exclaimed, "Bless the man, he's deaf as a post! What's the use of talking to him?"

TOWER OF BABEL

Question: What was the Tower of Babel?
Answer: Wasn't that where Solomon kept his wives?

TRACT

"Jehovah's Witnesses have tract me down!"

TRANSGRESSOR

The way of the transgressor is hard—to find out.

TROUBLES

A kindly country parson who had just married a young couple had a parting word for the groom: "Son, God bless you. You're at the end of all your troubles." A year later, the groom returned to the scene and moaned, "What a year I've gone through! And you're the man who told me I was at the end of my troubles."

"So I did, son," smiled the parson. "I just didn't tell you which end."

TRUTH

Truth may be stretched, but cannot be broken, and always gets above falsehood, as oil does above water.

Craft must have clothes, but truth loves to go naked.

TWEEDLE

A minister named Tweedle reluctantly refused a Doctor Of Divinity degree. He said that he'd rather be Tweedle dumb than Tweedle, D.D.

23rd PSALM

A lot of church members know the Twenty-third Psalm much better than they know the Shepherd.

A three-year-old version of the 23rd Psalm . . . "He leadeth me beside distilled water."

A young woman named Murphy was teaching a Sunday school class the 23rd Psalm. As the little voices chorused out, she seemed somewhere to detect a false note. She heard the children one by one until at last she came across one little boy who was concluding with the words, "Surely good Miss Murphy shall follow me all the days of my life."

TYPEWRITER

"I operate a typewriter by the biblical system."

"What is that?"

"The 'seek-and-ye-shall-find' system."

UMPIRES

The devil challenged St. Peter to a baseball game. "How can you win, Satan?" asked St. Peter. "All the famous ball-players are up here." "How can I lose?" answered Satan. "All the umpires are down here."

UNITARIAN

Is it true that if you're a Unitarian bigots burn a question mark on your lawn?

UNITED

1st Man: Are the members of your church united?

2nd Man: Yes.

1st Man: Praise the Lord for that.

2nd Man: I don't know about that. They're united because they are all frozen together.

USHER

The retiring usher was instructing his youthful successor in the details of his office. "And remember, my boy, that we have nothing but good, kind Christians in this church . . . until you try to put someone else in their pew."

VANITY

A young girl went to her pastor and confessed that she feared she had incurred the sin of vanity. "What makes you think that?" asked the minister. "Because every morning when I look in the mirror I think how beautiful I am."

"Never fear, my girl," was the reassuring reply. "That isn't a sin, it's only a mistake."

VEIL

A minister married a couple. The woman had on a veil and he could not see her face. After the ceremony, the man asked the minister, "How much do I owe you?"

"No charge," replied the minister.

"But I want to show my appreciation." So the man gave him fifty cents.

About that time the bride pulled off her veil, and the minister, looking at the bride, gave the man twenty-five cents change.

——■——

VICIOUS

"Best vicious for a Merry Christmas."

——■——

VOICE

The choir had come out of rehearsal. "Am I to assume that you do a lot of singing at home?" Bill Garrison asked a fellow choir member, Roy Greene.

"Yes, I sing a lot. I use my voice just to kill time," said Roy.

Bill nodded, "You certainly have a fine weapon."

VOLUNTEER

Volunteer work is when you have to explain to your kids that Daddy hasn't died. He just became a deacon of his church.

——■——

WICKED

Deacon: It says here, "The wicked flee when no man pursueth."

Pastor: "Yes, that's true, but they make much better time when somebody is after them."

——■——

WICKEDNESS

The way to wickedness is always through wickedness.

——■——

WINDED

Visitor: Your preacher is sure long winded.

Member: He may be long . . . but never winded.

WORSE

A pastor always used the phrase, "It might be worse," when some calamity would come his way. One day a friend said to him, "I've something to tell you, and you won't be able to use your favorite phrase. I dreamt last night that I died and went to hell." "It might be worse," said the preacher. "Man alive, how could it be worse?" "It might be true."

Index